Prologue

As a child at three years old my father was diagnosed with Multiple Sclerosis, a chronic disease of the central nervous system. This disease then proceeded to rip through our family.

Too young to remember how exactly this diagnosis impacted upon our family life. I do know however, dreams were lost, ambition halted and the shape of four lives changed forever.

In The Last Cake I aim to express hope and wisdom with the inevitable pain and loss. It is a book of my life, in extracts, my feelings, fears and emotions.

Facts and structure are true to life, names changed except those of my parents and my children, and some events, vague due to time and memory.

Whilst written partly as a tribute to my parents, the immense strength they both held to and the enormity of their suffering, The Last Cake is also entirely mine, touching on bereavement and loss, depression and desperation, physical abuse within relationships, alcohol addiction and guilt, immeasurable joy, love, laughter and hope.

Also I wish for some closure in writing this book. Some events, that even to this very day I find it almost impossible to live with. From the deepest darkest pain that still remains I hope for freedom.

I do however strive for happiness to shine from The Last Cake too, to make you laugh out loud, cry without control and some level of self-gratification to also enhance your life, in some small way.

Almost impossible to decide on a start and an ending, rather like an abstract painting of a life clear in front of you, yet distorted from the sides, colourful and glorious, incomprehensible but obvious.

It is not my intention to pass judgement upon any of the other people in this book, I leave you to make your own, keeping in mind that all events are purely from my perspective and not that of others. Many lives are shaped by events from their past, but that is their story not mine.

After much deliberation, with the pleasure of yourself and the necessity for myself to be understood, I chose a point in time, vivid in my mind, memory of detail and feelings as though yesterday. So from this point I take you by the hand, and lead you with me through my memories.

Now, more than anything I hope you enjoy reading The Last Cake as much as I have writing it. Emotional, and heartfelt, with every word.

I thank you in advance for reading.

Rosie Fenton

Chapter 1

I could hear Mum on the telephone downstairs in the hall, I couldn't make out the words, but I was sure it would be a telephone call to the Doctor. I dressed quickly, my mind racing, I knew Daddy wasn't too well last night, but not severe enough for the Doctor to visit I thought. Giving less attention than normal to my hair and the colour of my socks, I rushed downstairs.

Daddy slept in a single bed in what was once our dining room, commode in the corner and various contraptions that helped us look after him. Disabled and mostly bedridden with Multiple Sclerosis. Evil bastard of a disease, I hated the very name, and also felt weirdly guilty.

My breakfast was set out on the side in the kitchen as always, boiled egg, toast and milky coffee, always the same on a school day. Thomas, my older brother had already left for work.

I looked through to Daddy in his bed. "He's not well at all today darling, I've called the Doctor, he will be out later this morning" Mum spoke these words but they washed over me, something was different this time, he looked different, not just pale almost grey.

Mum was as normal really, she sat with him while I ate,

then helped me gather my school things. I went in to say goodbye and kissed my Daddy on the forehead, he could not reply to me, he tried but the words stayed in his throat.

I walked to the bus stop, trying to push away the pain burning inside me, the feeling of turning back, I knew I should go to school, Mum would want me to, so I must do as was expected.

At the bus stop I avoided conversation with the other village girls, we always waited in the same place, the boys in another, the school bus took us to the High School in the small, rather dreary town nearby.

Morning was really as any other, I couldn't concentrate however, my mind was with Daddy, willing him to get over what was obviously another infection. He was susceptible to infections of the bladder and kidney, usually with medication he quickly recovered back to what was normal for him. I loved my father with every part of me. I helped feed and clothe him, scratched his head, combed his hair and on occasion even gave him a shave. It was a role not only of daughter but also carer and best friend.

"Rosie is there any point to you being in my class this morning?" The voice of the history teacher cut through my thoughts. I looked up blankly from the back of the class, "you cock you have no idea" I thought, grateful then for the lunchtime bell.

Lunchtime came and went without event. I was already efficient in losing myself away from the crowd when necessary. French was a lesson I always enjoyed, a lovely old lady with the kind of face you would expect to see on any loving grandma was our teacher and I knew she had a soft spot for me. I was still distracted, hardly having time to open my book when there was a knock on the door, a pupil from another class appeared and spoke with the teacher, then they both looked at me in unison and the teacher called my name, I was wanted at the school office. I knew immediately, I struggled with my books, Kate sitting next to me, she helped me, I walked in a trance, the girl sent to collect me was kind, having no idea why I was called I remember her asking me if I had any cigarettes in my bag, saying she would hide them for me, I knew her but we were not close friends, her kindness stays in my memory.

I walked the corridor to the office alone, I wanted turn around, make it not real, make the day stop and rewind. The office door was ajar, only my Mum inside, sat in the far corner, she raised her head as she heard me, tears on her grief stricken face told me all my fears were true. I don't remember what happened next, how we got to the car, how we got home. I walked into the kitchen, blue painted walls and doors. I walked to his bed, I was allowed to see him before they came to take him away. My Mum left us, I don't remember my words or if I even had any, I can see his hand though, clearly in mine, white and cold, I held my Daddy's hand for the last time, I was 13 years old, he was only 37, my very best friend died on that day and my reason for everything was gone.

The next few days in my memory are simply just a blur, day into night into day into night. I know I had a desperate needing to stay strong for Mum as I imagined her hurt must be greater than mine, although I couldn't comprehend a greater pain than the one I felt. I shed no tears at school, not one, the minute I walked back through the door at home I found my grief impossible to contain, for my Mum I simply had to, so hours of solitude in my room was my only option.

As the funeral day approached it was decided that I was too young to attend, so my cousin who was the same age and myself were to attend school as usual on that day, then return to my house where there would be family members from Daddy's funeral.

I wasn't sure how I felt about this decision, looking back I am positive it wasn't the right one, although I understand it and the reasons behind it.

On the morning itself I walked to the bus stop as normal, as I approached Lucy my cousin walked towards me. You would have imagined that Lucy and I would be very close, cousins, same age living in the same village, but that was not the case. We shared the same circle of friends, but close we were not. On that morning however, she walked to meet me, we embraced, no words exchanged, none were needed.

Following an uneventful, almost impossible to endure day at school Lucy and I returned to my house. Aunts I hadn't seen before, familiar relatives I had no emotion for and my close family were all there to greet us. I wanted them gone, all gone. I had no idea of what to say, what emotion I was allowed to show let alone feel.

It was here, on this day, at the tender age of 13 that my unhealthy relationship with alcohol began.

We were a family where alcohol was readily available, from a young age we were allowed the occasional glass of wine, a tot of sherry of a Christmas time. On this day however I discovered it's ability to change your mood, your thought processes and emotions. So as the family chatted, some with tea, some with wine or something stronger, glasses were left unattended, so a young girl could easily partake in a sip or two from a stranded glass, it's numbing effect was most welcome! I believe my brother noticed but as Thomas was five and half years older than me, I think he just thought it cool at the time. Also gave ideal bargaining opportunity for the future!

Strange brother and sister relationship between Tom and myself. He was my big brother when it suited him to be so and on other occasions simply just a git, but then I think that is possibly normal sibling stuff.

After Daddy died it seemed to be mostly Mum and I at home, Tom being that bit older was out most evenings, we ate together as a family but pretty much that was it.

Another wonderful and very prominent person in my life was my Nan. I adored her, we spent many hours together when Mum was working, which she returned to doing after we lost Daddy. My Nan was not an educated women, she worked hard as a cleaner in our village, nearly into her seventies. She was a marvel, always happy and laughing, my Grand dad had died three years ago so she lived alone in a cottage on the village green, very much in need of renovation, with no bathroom at all and a small back room that could only loosely be described as a kitchen. No central heating and an outside toilet. Yet she never complained. My dear Nan what a friend she was. She spent a number of hours with Mum and me at home, calling round every evening. Always for Sunday lunch and a weekly bath. Despite our grief we were relatively happy, on the surface at least. Insular, however.

My relationship with my Mum was always a close one; I knew unequivocally that I was her world. She always favoured me over Tom which on occasion left me feeling quite uncomfortable and without doubt made our bond as brother and sister fragile.

This also meant that Mum confided in me, she wasn't as close to her own Mum even as I was, she had good work colleagues and I believe she spoke to a couple of those on a personal level but in the main it was me she would turn to. As she did on a day within the same year as losing Daddy, it was a school day, that I remember, I was getting ready and she came and sat on my bed, no tears but serious, I sat next to her and she just said it "Rosie you do know I've got it too don't you? MS" "Yes of course I do" was my reply, and I did. We hugged and continued with our day.

At school, I remember feeling hurt and angry, what I had been told was not a revelation, I did know, or thought it possible, but to hear Mum say it was totally devastating, I could not let her see that though. I stood in the science lab, it was on the second floor, watching the other kids, and I felt so alone in this impossible hurt that had landed upon me again. I shed a single tear and sat at my desk as the others started to filter in. I was boiling inside, I wanted to scream as loud as anyone could scream. I sat paying no attention to our teacher, he was one of the better ones too, saw children not numbers, he noticed my disinterest and came over to me, put his hands on the desk and leaned over, I do not recall one single word he said to me, but there was his tie, just hanging in front of me, like an invitation, I picked up the scissors on my desk and without a word I cut it off!

He said nothing, just returned to the front of the class, asked for quiet as there was a certain amount of sniggering, removed the remainder of his tie and continued with the lesson. I just sat there during the whole period, looking out the window, so deep in my thoughts. Science over and the teacher asked me to stay behind. I told him everything, sobbed as I did so. After a short silence he put his hand on my shoulder, "you may go to lunch now, and Rosie, make sure you eat something".

The tie incident wasn't mentioned again. I didn't talk of Mum's illness at school again.

Mum and I holidayed together. As I grew up these holidays took us abroad, only to Europe, but wonderful holidays. Drinking alcohol quickly became the norm for Mum and me. She allowed me to drink way too much on occasion although I am positive in the knowledge that she had no conception of the damage this was to do. It was on these holidays that I noticed Mum's symptoms more obviously, all I could feel was sorrow and helped her in every way possible to make things easier for her. I can't imagine how hard it was for her to accept after nursing the husband she adored to his death with this evil, debilitating disease, to face the same fate herself. I drank to forget.

At home also from the age of about 17, drinking alcohol at home every evening became normality. Mum made her own wine, not very spectacular stuff, and never allowed the desired time to mature, I doubt very much that it held much strength. None the less, alcohol it was, and drank with alarming frequency for such a young girl, or any adult for that matter.

Also, by this age and younger, I was finding some comfort in controlling food intake. Life seemed to have taken me along a very hurtful path and one that I had no control over. Food however was extremely easily to control and the results of disappearing weight brought with it extra attention and the pity that somehow, for reasons to this day I don't understand, I needed.

As my Mum's condition worsened, things at home became more difficult, I don't recall any conversation with Tom about Mum's health at this point but he was beginning to notice and ask questions. Mum also visited the family GP in regard to her symptoms but she was dismissed as being irrational due to Daddy's illness, it was thought she simply read too much into the physical difficulties she was having. We both knew that was not the case though, when you live with a person and are closer to them than any other you see things that the world does not see. She was unbelievably strong, worked fulltime as a telephonist in a large retail store in Rugby, another town which was close to us. Tom and I were extremely well cared for any our home was always kept in good repair. Even the garden was immaculate, not a huge garden, but one of a good size,, three bed roomed semi-detached with a long garden. In the summer Mum was in the garden every evening until dusk. As she was at this time fighting a chronic illness she must've been exhausted, she never said so, she was happy and just a wonderful person who certainly did not deserved the cards that life had dealt to her.

I was relatively popular at school, always had friends and boyfriends too as we got older. Inside I felt the opposite, always self-conscious, worried by what others thought of me but craved attention and solitude in equal measures. At parties and events, I was always the one who drank the most, but I loved to dance, eighties music was good for dancing, and I felt happier dancing in a crowd a wash with alcohol, I could feel free in that environment, rather than in conversation with my friends. One friend was always so loyal and extremely special to me, to this day Kate and I are the very best of friends.

On leaving school, I chose to take a college course, Visual Arts Foundation Course. Photography was my love, had been from an early age. I recall on many a holiday with Mum, dragging her miles just take the shot I had to take! It was as a photographer that I hoped to make my career.

First days are always tricky and first day at College in Northampton was no different. My fellow students were a fantastic and interesting bunch, we all of course shared similar passion, some in photography, some art and some drama, and I have to say drama students are an extremely unique lot!

I made friends quickly though, no animosity with any of them. It is a time of my life that I remember fondly. I had passed my driving test, Mum had bought me a little blue mini which I completely adored. Weekends were spent mostly with my Nan while Mum worked on a Saturday and Sundays were the day for chores. For set tasks Mum paid me enough money to keep me going along with babysitting jobs that I also did, helping at home with the decorating, cleaning and gardening also helped Mum as her symptoms were progressing quite rapidly.

As I approached the end of the first year of my two year course at college, it was obvious that I would easily achieve exam grades necessary for me to then take a diploma course at university in Luton. The reality of this however would involve either a lengthy journey there and back on a daily basis or a move away from home. I gave this hours of thought before reaching the decision that, as much as I longed to follow my dream, I could not move that far from home. Poor Mum was becoming more and more unsteady, hurting herself on an almost daily basis. Work was enormously hard for her by now, she continued though. The thought of being so far away just filled me with dread. So I ended my college course a year early choosing to seek employment instead.

However I had no direction in which to go, work was easy to find then and a number of options were open to me. One of these seemed far simpler than the others, not the most lucrative however. A position was available for a nanny to a titled family in the village. The main house of the family was glorious, sitting in an elevated position on my favourite road out of the village, this house or Hall as it was called; I had longed to live in for as long as I could remember. The position was at the farmhouse across the road from the Hall. I knew the name of the people and their faces, villages are like that, my Mum's neighbour's sister was a cleaner at the farmhouse and her I did know, and knew her as a lovely gentle lady. So after a phone call the position was mine. Two children, one a toddler and the other just a baby. Now, I had never even held a baby before, the lady of the house showed me around. The basics in child care were covered and that was pretty much that! I was ridiculously nervous which she dismissed, and within a couple of days left alone with these two very young children. I believe that is a daunting task for anyone let alone a young girl with no experience and a very difficult home life to contend with. I muddled through is the best way to describe it. Two mornings of the week when the lovely lady was there to clean were great, she taught me way more than the mother found time to do.

Six months in total I managed to stay in this poorly paid emotionally draining position. Those six months included domestic disasters that I hid, broken valuable kitchen ware and a situation with chicken shit in the best room. I had to leave, the stress was immense, I found the

Mum intimidating to the point of rudeness and little gratitude that was desperately needed to boost my confidence. Of the children though I had become very fond, so my last day there was bittersweet. I was extremely relieved to arrive home that night knowing I would never have to go back and vowed categorically to never be a nanny again!

The next few months I spent at home, job searching, interviews at various different jobs came to no avail and I was beginning to get frustrated. I needed to work. Mum's wage could not sustain both of us especially with my by now quite expensive drinking habit.

So much to my annoyance I was to take up yet another Nanny position. Very different to the first however, this family had money and lots of it. Their house was grand and like none I had ever been inside, unless there was a neon sign saying Hotel above the door! Older father, younger Mother, I remember thinking on many occasion that all the money in the world could not bring me to climb into bed with that great monstrosity to land on top of me, hideous man!

They were obnoxious, demanding and people I could have no respect for. The children were older though, one school age and the other nursery age. There was also a daily cleaner and a groom to giggle with and we did, quite often, and at their expense. With this job also came a larger salary and a company car in the shape of a land rover! I felt quite the bee's knees driving round in that!

During this time I started with what was really my first

serious boyfriend. There had been a few before, one I was extremely fond of and one I was extremely sexual with and a few others not worth a mention. Andrew Grant was from the village, a school year above me, my first grown up, adult relationship. He rented a room and worked in a bank, so we had money and a place to be alone, no more shagging in cars, now that was a relief. At the beginning we had a lovely relationship, he liked to spoil me on regular occasion and was also quite willing to spend time with me at home. Sunday lunch with my Mum was something I did not want to let go of.

Also during this time Mum's multiple sclerosis was confirmed after a week-long stay at a hospital in Oxford. I went with her for the initial appointment and then visited her on every evening of her stay and Andrew took me to each of those visits bar one when I went with Tom. So very hard to see my dear dear Mum who was still only in her forties in so much pain following invasive procedures and to leave her there alone every night. Andrew was very supportive during all of this.

Mum still returned to work after a few weeks and coped with her illness with amazing strength, I was in awe of my Mum and would do anything to prevent her further turmoil.

So when at the end of my eighteenth year I fell pregnant with Andrew's baby, given that my Mum was very old fashioned in that respect and had no knowledge of our sexual activity, I felt no choice but to terminate my pregnancy, never telling my Mum about it at all. On the day before my nineteenth birthday I went into

Northampton General Hospital and ended a little life, so very sad I was and alone in this grief as Andrew was relieved that my mother's feelings had been pivotal in this decision. He would not have supported me had my decision been the opposite.

I got particularly drunk on my twentieth birthday, Andrew was most unkind and mocking of my feelings towards to loss of our baby.

In the Christmas of the same year we decided to get married. Never lived together first just decided to marry. I knew this would make Mum extremely happy and proud that I was for all intents and purposes I virgin bride, to be married in white in the village church. The same church I had been christened and confirmed in. The same church where my Mother and Father had married and many family members previous. The same church where my Father's funeral had taken place. The funeral I was not allowed to attend.

Chapter 2

Still working as a nanny for the rich and ruthless, I had no plans to leave, it was far from the perfect job, but it was okay. I worked most Saturday mornings which was probably the most annoying part as it broke into our weekend quite substantially. Governing our Friday night plans and also those of Saturdays. It was on one of my rostered Saturdays that we planned a trip into Northampton in the afternoon, leaving as early as possible to take in lunch at one of the growing number of Pizzerias, well the mother of the children I worked for was late returning from a shopping trip, obviously I could not leave until she returned so this delay in our plans was out of my control.

Andrew as on so many occasions it seemed by now thought otherwise. When he collected me he was somewhat fractious to say the least, I decided to say as little as possible, sit in the passenger seat and quietly nurse my hangover hoping his mood would soon pass. It didn't. By the time we had reached Northampton his mood was dangerous, we struggled to park the car (my fault), we had no time for lunch (my fault) and everywhere we went was busy, of course, again, my fault. It got to the point where he was simply ranting at me, nothing I said was even heard, he started then to just ignore me, strutting up the main street like a complete twat. I was angry by now, so, I started to drop behind, then, and I have no idea what made me do this but I dived into a shop, quickly as I could coming out of an entrance on the opposite side, so a different street. I practically ran down the road, I knew by now I was on my way to the train station!

I boarded the next train for Rugby, where my Mum was at work. No mobile phones of course in the late eighties, Andrew had no idea where I had gone at this stage, I was quite smug with my escaping skills.

I sat on the train holding my finger with my engagement ring on it. I remember thinking "why does he treat me this way? He says he loves but is just bloody unkind" A conversation I had with Daddy came to mind, I could ask my father anything and one day after junior school, I came in straight to see Daddy as I always did "Daddy you okay? Need anything? What's a cunt?" He told me what it was and also that it was a swear word for a thoroughly despicable person, he also said that no decent person would ever use that word.

From where I sat, looking out the window of that train I thought that word aptly described my fiancé that day.

Andrew and I chose for our wedding, a date in September of the following year. It was very exciting choosing the dress and Kate was to be my only bridesmaid. Kate's dress was to be made by a friend of hers, mine I chose from a little boutique within the department store where Mum worked so we did get a considerable discount. The dress was gorgeous, pure white with a fitted body to show off my ample bust!

Fitted at the waist with a meringue of a skirt.

I felt like a princess in that dress. I thought that despite his spiky temper he was my prince.

The months preceding the wedding, were fractious at times. Family problems with who to and who not to invite. Mum was very proud and insisted upon paying for everything, Andrew's Mother also wanted to help and was more than slightly disgruntled when Mum was adamant to fund the entire day herself.

Tom was to give me away in the absence of Daddy, which hurt me so much, I would have given anything to be holding his arm walking down that aisle, I had real concerns about how I was going to hold it together without him.

As the day approached I was also extremely worried as to how Mum would cope with the day, physically and emotionally. Closer to me than anyone, she expressed on numerous occasions how much she was going to miss me. I tried as best I could to reassure her that as we would still be living in the village I should be able to pop and see her most days and cook Sunday roast for her and Nan myself in my own home. That I looked forward to very much.

Andrew however, was expressing his feelings very clearly that once we were married I would belong to him and we would not have time for my Mother every day and it would be unreasonable of her to expect that. I tried to explain though how hard this would be for her and for not to forget that she was fighting a chronic illness.

That illness was forefront in my mind for the day itself, Mum had a variety of issues she dealt with on a daily basis, regarding, balance, tremors, standing for any length of time and the toilet. It was not going to be an easy day for her and there was nothing I could do to make it so.

I felt so torn and we were not even married. Soon became clear that this was going to be much the same as my life already had been, where my feeling needed to be kept away in a safe place while I took care of everybody else's.

In the middle of all these preparations, I was at work one day, just a normal day, the boy was at school and the little girl nursery. I was given a number of chores to do in a town 10 miles or so from the nursery. Collecting items from a dry cleaners and a large order from the butchers there, amongst other things. I was mindful of the time, not wanting to be late collecting the little girl. I rushed to the car (an old spare car as the Land Rover was being serviced) piled everything in and took off. I had to pull out from a side road on to the main road, turning right so crossing the line of traffic. I looked, I know I looked, but I pulled out and from round the corner another car hit me, sent me flying, both cars a wreck. I was bruised and shaken but not seriously hurt. It did however make me think about the responsibility of the job, I was often driving with their children in my care. What if an accident happened and one of the children was hurt, that would be my fault. I took some time off after the accident, which they were fine with, but didn't pay me! I decided I couldn't return. I just felt so anxious about taking their children out in the car I could no longer do it.

Andrew supported this decision, having never been happy about the weekend hours. This time I was even more determined to find a job of a different nature.

I applied to many of the banks and building societies, and was asked for an interview by the same bank that Andrew worked for just in a different town. He wasn't overjoyed by this, which I couldn't understand, but finally agreed I could go to the interview. Well, they offered me a position as a junior cashier, I was so thrilled, so was Mum, and very proud too. When Andrew came round to pick me up that evening I was so excited to tell him. Initially he just didn't react, said nothing at all, I was confused to say the least. He then bit by bit came up with reasons why I should not take the position. The travelling distance was too long, I would be 'out of my depth' in a banking environment, he talked me out of it. I turned it down. Completely deflated I sat with my Nan mostly for a few days, Mum and Andrew both at work, being with Nan always cheered me up. Then, not sure what day it was, but I remember Mum and I sitting watching television, in the sitting room, with dinner on our laps, salad with French bread, it's funny the little things that stay in your memory. The phone rang, I got up to answer, it was my Optician, I had known him since I was a child, he had that day tested the eyes of the bank manager who offered me the job. The Optician had talked with him about needing to find a new receptionist, the bank manager told him of me saying "she won't work for me, maybe she will for you". He told me what was involved and would I like to come in and discuss it with him. I did. I started as an Optical receptionist and assistant the following Monday.

Neither of us were concerned about an evening reception, I had this perfect image in my head of our lovely small family reception in the afternoon and then changing into a little cream suit which I had bought months in advance, and whisking off in a wedding car to the airport for our honeymoon, somewhere exotic, where we would drink champagne in the sunshine. It was the only part of our day that we totally agreed on. So the church was booked for eleven to be followed by a family reception at a small local hotel. The wedding car to the airport was a grey taxi and our exotic location was Jersey in Channel Islands.

Although not exotic, with the money we had Jersey was a good location, also held very fond memories for me.

It was Jersey that we went to when I was a child, to a hotel for disabled people and their families. The first time we went, we were all apprehensive. There were disabled adults and children with a range of disabilities, physically and mentally. I shared a bedroom with Mum and Daddy and Tom had a small single room near to ours. Our room had everything in it that Daddy needed for his care, special mattress and lifting apparatus.

The first meal was a challenge, I was only 10 at the time, we all ate at the same time in a main hall, seated around one large table. Opposite me was a boy, I couldn't tell his age and he was severely handicapped with Spina bifida, as his mother tried to feed him, he dribbled and made horrific screaming noises. I found this awful, hardly ate any of my own meal. But as the week progressed we spent a lot of time with all the other guests, the Sunshine Coaches took us to various places round the island, both day and evening too. By the end of the week I was extremely fond of the little boy, playing with him on the floor many times I realised the emotions from this wonderful child were all expressed through his eyes. He and many of the other guests left warmth and love in my memory. It was a massive learning curve for a 10 year old but one I am so grateful for. We returned to the same hotel twice more and were booked to go in the year we lost Daddy. It was completely heart breaking to cancel that trip.

So the first week of our Honeymoon was to be in Jersey, having been before I chose the Hotel. One that I remembered as being in a beautiful location and one of the best we could afford with our budget.

The second week was to be in Cornwall, where the family I had worked for owned a cottage and they said that we could have it for that week, as a their wedding gift to us.

I wanted to go and see Mum on the weekend in the middle of our Honeymoon, as we would be returning home to collect the car and quickly wash and dry clothes. Andrew was livid about this, saying it was completely inappropriate! I never really worked out who was right and who was wrong. Or if there even was I right or wrong. I just felt, my Mum as not a well woman would love a short visit from us and I wanted to go. We did go, but I was made to feel very guilty and torn once again.

I was not allowed a hen night! Andrew was adamant! I was so shocked and really cross, how he dare dictate to me like that. He dug his heals right in though, he wasn't having a stag do and I was not having a hen do, over his dead body! I was disgusted and very disappointed too. I went with his wishes, telling the girls at work, and my friends that I didn't want to do anything. I did want to, very much.

Andrew was starting to worry me as the Wedding day came closer; he seemed more controlling, saying I would 'belong' to him, this just sounded weird to me. We were going to be a partnership, lovers and best friends. I certainly wasn't a possession but that was exactly what I was beginning to feel like.

I lay in bed at night begging for guidance from Daddy. Of course there was none. I told nobody of these fears and resolved to continue with our plans. Things had gone too far for me to ruin everything just because of a few little niggles. Mum had spent a fortune, things were all in place. I was to be a bride, stunning and lovely. It was going to be perfect. I would be loved, adored and taken care of for the rest my life. Andrew was simply stressed by it all. Wanting perfection for our day as I.

I woke up in my bed, in my bedroom for what I believed would be the last time. Mixed emotions and massive hangover, hairdresser due shortly. I was excited though, and still believed I was doing the right thing. I loved Andrew, it had to be right.

Hair looked gorgeous, quite a task in itself, I wasn't blessed with good hair. Kate arrived and Mum seemed okay, I knew she was worried, about needing the toilet more than anything, it is a major concern, bladder control when you don't have it.

Kate looked beautiful in her dress, there was something in her eyes that day that told me she wasn't so sure I was doing the right thing. We were both young, still only 20 and I know she didn't like some of Andrew's ways, and sensed she was worried for me. Never the less she was every bit the perfect bridesmaid and put me at ease having her and Mum with me before the church.

Of the actually service itself I remember very little. I remember another one of my cousin's Josie, older than me and didn't live in the village, so only ever saw her at family occasion such as this, she turned and looked at me as Tom walked me down the aisle, a lovely warm genuine smile. Then Mum with tears in her eyes at the front. I didn't cry, too nervous, that many eyes, all on me and my hangover, I was keen to get that part out of the way. Looking back I question that emotion.

I remember the photographer, as a keen photographer myself I had insisted we had a professional of good reputation, as after the day the photographs would be to keep, forever, show our children and hang on the walls of our home. This however meant that we were an absolute age outside the Church, in every pose possible.

Andrew was getting exasperated I could tell, I was silently wishing that he would just be happy, for us both on such a wonderful day in our lives. Myself I really needed the toilet and a drink!

The Hotel for our reception was literally a minute's drive from the Church. As we arrived, as we requested, two large Southern Comfort and lemonade's waited for us on the bar. Dreadful drink, but I loved it back then.

This of course was followed by much champagne and in my case little food. Visiting the toilet in a wedding dress such as mine was is not the easiest thing to do and when you drink great volumes you also pee the same. Obviously I had to keep control, Andrew really would not have been impressed had I not, and I too wanted to stay with my day and not lose it.

It was a lovely day on the whole, everything went to plan. Speeches short and sweet, my brother did the best he could and I was proud of him. I was too immensely proud of Mum, she looked beautiful, and poised throughout the entire day, I know how emotional it was for her. My heart cried out to make her happy. Kate as always was just wonderful, we had a moment and hugged in the toilet at some point. I was happy, very happy.

At the time for us to leave, Andrew and I changed in one of the upstairs bedrooms and collected our luggage for the first week of our honeymoon. I was looking exactly as I imagined. Short cream linen suit with brown suede shoes and matching bag. I could not stop looking at the rings on my finger. I was determined to be the very best wife that I could be. Fully embraced my new role, the evidence of this was the smile on my face.

I had a long hug with Mum, that was tearful, I was so aware of what she would be feeling and that she now would be living alone. Thomas was already married to Jane, lovely girl from the next village although they now lived in the same village as us, so Mum still had them close and of course my Nan, although truth be told she irritated Mum in many ways. Mostly though because for the whole of my Mum's childhood, as the youngest of three, the other two boys which Nan had very much favoured and that rejection stayed with my Mum her whole life even though Nan loved her dearly.

Andrew and I boarded the plane to Jersey, I was still buzzing with excitement. It's a very short flight to Jersey and as Andrew would be driving our hire car almost immediately on landing, he did not drink. My small bottle of white wine did not please him one little bit, but for goodness sake, there's only two glasses in those tiny bottles and it was my wedding day!

It was early evening before we arrived at our hotel. Andrew said "it looked okay from the outside" his enthusiasm was overwhelming! I remained in my happy wedding day bubble. We had matching luggage with our initials on them, I even had one of those cute little vanity cases, matching of course!

We checked in, the staff were lovely, very welcoming and said for us to come down when ready for dinner.

When we got to the room, we opened the door and inside we found a normal size double bed, very average in décor with a rather small en suite. We had asked for a king-sized bed. Andrew was completely livid, I tried to make light of it, tried to remind him how perfect the day had been and that this really was a minor thing, not worth getting upset about. He pushed past me and stormed downstairs to reception to complain. I sat down heavily on the bed, looked at the rings on my finger, then tucked my hands under my thighs out of sight and cried.

The hotel managed to upgrade our room the following day. Our wedding night was ruined, but not by them in my eyes, by Andrew and his temper. Growing up I never once heard my father shout, Mum yes, on occasion, but never Dad and he certainly never said anything unkind to our Mum. Once again I pushed it to the back of my mind and vowed wholeheartedly to enjoy this gorgeous week in beautiful Jersey, I couldn't wait to visit some of the places holding those oh so precious memories. To show Andrew all the places that meant the very most to me.

The week, seemed short. We toured around the island, taking in the sights, eating lunches in country pubs and dressed for our evening meal every night in our hotel. We shopped for souvenirs. I took nearly one hundred photographs. Taking one of these photo's on a beach one day, the sand was wet, so I crouched rather than kneel and wet my jeans, Andrew made a comment that my hand was shaking "no, it's just I'm cold" I quickly replied, thinking "my God he's looking for it, for signs that I too will get MS" it was something that was always in my mind, there is a genetic link, but to hear him say that, and not in a soft concerned manor, sharp, almost like an accusation. That hurt.

One evening we drove out to La Corbiere lighthouse, it's one of the famous images of Jersey, the lighthouse, it's the most south westerly point of the island and is beautiful of evening.

We would drive here of evening as a family when I was a child. This point was a particular favourite of my father's. When his health was better, Daddy was a painter, oil on canvas and extremely good at it too. Many of his paintings were sold, he exhibited in local exhibitions. His dream was to live one day in Cornwall and make a living selling his paintings of the local area. This lighthouse was one he wished he had been well enough to paint, but he had lost the use of his hands by the time we visited Jersey. His talent had kept him painting longer than was imaginable, creating glorious pictures long after his hands were efficient with a knife and fork or able to dial the numbers on a telephone. He steadied one hand with the other resting against the canvas with Mum or I, holding his head steady to complete his last few works and the signatures again done by Mum or me.

So that evening to be there again with Andrew was so important to me. As were so many places we visited during that week. He seemed oblivious.

Chapter 3

After both weeks of our honeymoon were over we settled into married life together. We rented a house in the village which belonged to Andrew's mother who had moved away to a different area, she was unsure of her long-term plans for the property, but it was our understanding that for the time being anyway she had no plans to sell.

We decorated, hung pictures and photographs and very soon it was feeling much like home. Andrew still working for the bank, and myself enjoying my work at the opticians.

Happy we were, although Andrew's standards were high and his expectation of me the same. With working full time, I was required to keep an immaculate house, have a home cooked meal prepared every evening and maintain active regular bedroom activity!

For myself I found priority in all those things but more importantly helping and spending as much time with Mum as I could. Her MS was accelerating at an alarming rate and she was lonely too. I found myself spread pretty thinly and with no me time, ever.

My twenty-first Birthday was approaching, Andrew would doubtless buy me a perfect expensive piece of jewellery. The night itself though I wanted to spend with Mum, I didn't want a party of any kind, just a lovely meal out for the three of us… oh it was becoming already such a balancing act, keeping everyone happy and avoiding conflict which I would do where possible.

We did go out for dinner, the three of us. Nan was never one for pubs or restaurants else I would have wanted her there too. We went to the same hotel as our wedding reception, lovely food as always, well from what I can remember. Andrew bought a bottle of champagne, wine with the meal and Mum bought Brandy's for afterwards, her and I were tipsy, giggly and enjoying ourselves. Andrew was judgemental of everything I did by this time. We went home early. I sat alone at midnight, on the floor of our lovely sitting room in our four bed roomed detached house, wine in hand, crying silent tears. I never thought being twenty-one would feel that way.

I began to feel lonely in my marriage, my frequent visits to Mum the frequent cause for argument. I had always kept pets, we always had a dog growing up. So I found the courage to discuss this with Andrew, saying maybe just a small dog, from a rescue centre, a puppy would not be right as we both worked fulltime. He wasn't completely against the idea, saying he had always liked Labradors, "Oh no Andrew, too big, and they need so much exercise that wouldn't be right for us" he walked off, no more was said.

My dear Mum was struggling to work fulltime, it was perfectly clear to Tom and I that really she shouldn't be working at all. Stubborn and fiercely independent was Mum though. One morning at work I had a phone call from Mum's work saying she had had a fall, she was okay and someone had taken her home. I left work immediately. When I got to her she was sitting in the chair downstairs, she told me what had happened and that it had been mutually agreed that she should take some time off work. I was relieved but worried at the same time, this fuck damn awful disease, she didn't deserve this, it was so unfair. We talked for some time discussing ways that we could all help her more. Tom called round, as he often did on his way home from work. He was pleased to help with the garden and taking the bins out. I was to do the weekly shop for her and Nan, also take over the care of Daddy's grave, which I visited regularly anyway. That evening I cooked for Mum, Andrew and myself at her house, she felt sore, bless her, from the fall and the usual painful crap that MS likes to dish out on a daily basis. I hugged her hard that night when we were leaving to go home, I loved this strong beautiful woman so much, I couldn't lose her too, I just couldn't.

Mum stayed off work, she never returned. Still, she was well enough to care for herself on a daily basis, with extra help with the big things for my brother and I, Nan too helped, she was very fit and healthy for a woman approaching eighty! Work however was just no longer an option and I was aware that she resented losing that part of her life, as anybody would.

Things at home were fine, I felt under scrutiny somehow though, constantly belittled by Andrew over trivial things.

Then one night he said he would be late home, not giving a reason, just said he would be an hour or so with something he had to do. I made sure the house was immaculate and casserole in the oven for his return. I was in the sitting room when he came in, he came straight to me with a bundle of black Labrador puppy in his arms. So shocked, but kind of delighted and kind of annoyed all at the same time. The puppy he said was mine, I could name him, he was all mine. This of course was to make up for the fact that he had gone directly against my wishes and bought the very kind of puppy I did not want!

I loved the fellow though, called him Rory, and he did make me happy with his unconditional simpleness.

With the addition of Rory to my life did come an extra set of chores and responsibilities. I worked the closest to our village so it was me who had to race home every lunchtime to feed and let him out. I loved walking him though, hours we spent in the fields that dog and I. Gave me space and thinking time. I could take him to Mum's so that was nice and easy too, two birds with one stone! So really although he wasn't exactly what I wanted, he was a joy and I soon loved him very much.

After Christmas, our first together as a married couple, fell Andrew's Birthday, he decided we would stay at home and invite his best friend and partner round for dinner. I had no problem with this, I could cook and loved to do so. I planned a three course dinner, including some of Andrew's favourite foods and the correct wine to accompany each course.

On the day, they arrived late afternoon, we all started drinking early, I was the only one drinking wine before the meal, a little nervous too, anxious for everything to be perfect, I drank more than I should and by the end of the night I was quite frankly rat arsed!

The couple decided it best they went home, obviously and understandably uncomfortable with the atmosphere in the house between Andrew and I. You would imagine wouldn't you, that if your partner did over indulge on such an occasion, whilst not being thrilled, you would still just help them to bed. Andrew oh no, married only four months, once we were alone, he grabbed me by the throat, with both hands. I sobered mighty quickly and was terrified, I made towards the front door, opened it, planning to run up the village to Mum's, then realising I didn't have my keys turned on the doorstep, Andrew was standing there, the look on his face was one I had never seen before, I froze, we had two steps up to our front door from the concrete drive, he pushed me backwards down the steps. I hit that concrete with a smack, I lay for a minute making sure everything still worked, a pushed myself upwards to a sitting position facing the front door, Andrew stood there, his expression steal, coldly and calmly he said to me "get back in this house now or you never will" I tried to find some strength, my mind was racing and my head hurt and my back. I pulled myself up, sat briefly on the bottom step, then went back in the house. Andrew went straight upstairs. I curled up on the hearth rug with Rory and slept right there.

I was woke at sunrise by Rory, most excited to find him next to me. I grabbed his lead, we went off down the field, not a work day thank goodness, we were gone some time. During my walk on that crisp January morning I decided that I was most certainly partly to blame for events of the previous night. Part of me from inside screamed you know this wrong. I silenced that voice. My marriage was important to me, I didn't want to be a failure. Mostly though I thought of my dearest Mum, I could not let her down, the beautiful wedding she had given us, paid with by money she didn't have. Her illness too was fuelled by stress. I must go back, be a good wife and try harder to do so. I looked up "Daddy please guide me through this, I wish you were here, I love you".

Wiped away the tears, walked home and made Andrew a cooked breakfast. He came down into the kitchen, my heart was beating almost out of my chest! " I made you breakfast" his expression was hard to read "Rosie don't get drunk like that again" I was about to reply then he just picked up his breakfast and walked through to the table. Nothing more was said.

In the spring of that year, Andrew's mother decided that she wanted to sell the property we were living in. It was a complete shock, many heated telephone conversations took place between Andrew and his mother. Her mind was set, so we had to start house hunting.

Our village was like many, with few properties affordable to a first time buyer. We viewed lots of properties, with Andrew's position in the bank we were fortunate to be offered a mortgage with reasonable terms, despite that we were limited with funds and as we thought we had to leave our village. We chose a small two bed semi in the small town nearest to the village, the same town I worked in. The house was nice, but very much smaller and on an estate, something neither of us were enamoured with.

For myself, there was also the massive concern of moving further away from Mum, albeit only a few miles. Also felt deep sorrow for moving away from Daddy's resting place, from our village home, I could see the graveyard from the spare bedroom window, and would often sit on the bed there, looking over and having a moment of thoughts of the father I loved so much, the father who never complained, the man who would never have raised his hand to his wife.

There was a marked downturn in our marriage on moving to that little house. The pressure on me to be wifey perfect grew as did the shortness of Andrew's temper. His control of me was greater than ever. My friendship with Kate was almost lost as he would not allow me any time with friends, so we drifted apart. He took to controlling our sex life in an intolerable way, he started taking me when I was sleeping, I would on many occasion wake to find him on top of me. This he always insisted I instigated. So one night I stayed awake pretending to sleep. As I thought he roughly pulled my legs apart, removed my tampon and forced himself inside, when he realised I was weeping, I begged him to stop telling him I knew I had done nothing to arouse him or show any sexual intent, he did not stop, the opposite, he bashed away hard, bruising my arms to keep me in place.

Afterwards he still strongly maintained it was only what I did that made him hurt me.

He then on a regular basis took me when he wanted, whether I was willing or not, whether I struggled or not, whether I cried or not. This took away from me my desire to be intimate with him at all.

I was living a private hell, I told nobody, confided in no one.

Close to our little house was a pub which we started to frequent on a quiz night and occasionally at other times and sometimes to eat. Being only a short walk away the quantity of alcohol consumed was not an issue. It became a very big issue between us though. My drinking had always angered Andrew greatly, but the less he understood of why I felt the need to lose myself in drink, the more I drank. He took to handling me very roughly, physically throwing me to the floor. Holding my arms and legs so hard they bruised. The sexual assault increased. Always held to blame, I truly didn't know what to believe, was my behaviour so terrible that I deserved these beatings? and rape within marriage was that acceptable too?. I questioned myself as much as him. All I did know was that I was desperately unhappy, my Mum was worsening in front of my eyes and I was powerless to help her. My only friend was that bottle.

I always maintained a perfect public front. Never drinking during the day. Working hard and being well respected at the Opticians. Caring well for Mum and being a good friend to her. Our house was always immaculate. Food well prepared and beautifully presented. I rarely drank to excess in front of family members and never drank to the point that I lost control of what I was doing or thinking. I wasn't flirtatious when we were out, humorous yes, that has always been another marvellous self-defence of mine, my quick wit has saved me from a difficult situation many a time. Another thing I inherited from Daddy, my super sense of humour. It doesn't however save you much from a husband who pulls apart your very being, missing no opportunity to berate you.

Now, it came to our attention, exactly how I don't recall, that a small bungalow had come up for sale back in our village. The bungalow was owned by two young people we both knew, India a lovely girl from my year at school, a village girl too, my Mum knew her parents, and her soon to be ex husband, not such a nice chap, I remember being quite shocked to hear of those two together in the first place. Both Andrew and I were keen to move back, I believed things could improve greatly if we could return to village life. Well the sale was all very soon in place, our little house sold quickly and India removed theirs from the agents so a simple private sale could take place.

In no time at all we were packing up our little house into boxes, theirs empty already and everything for the first time in a while seemed positive.

Mum was overjoyed at our return to the village, she bought us a brand new cooker as a house warming present, double oven belling, I never forgot that cooker, best one I ever had!

The bungalow inside was only slightly more spacious than our little house, but it had a lovely little private garden, driveway and garage, in a most perfect location. I could walk to Mum and to my Nan's. The fields were close, the graveyard was close. It was like coming home. We still continued to go to the town pub on quiz night. I loved those nights out. It was my only social life. Many different and diverse characters you find in any pub and this one no different and I thoroughly loved being part of the team we played with every week. Andrew did not fit in so well, he was not shall we say a typical bloke and thought of himself as above the rest which often meant he got the piss taken right out of him. Daphne became his nickname, which I quietly had to snigger at.

It was after an evening out, one where I had not drank to excess. Behaved impeccably and left the pub when Andrew wished, which was often before the evening had finished. On returning home his mood was foul. I tried to sort Rory as quickly as possible to get to bed and avoid the conflict that was so obviously brewing within him. I failed and he violated me. So badly that he made me bleed. I was not only sore but bereft. Our move to that little bungalow I believed would save us. It didn't. I now faced a new set of questions that I needed to ask myself and answer honestly and for right reasons. I didn't sleep. The following day was difficult at work, friends noticed I was significantly down compared with my normal sunny state. I brushed it under the 'concerned for Mum umbrella' and lost myself in the upstairs storeroom sorting spectacle cases.

I knew I had to be strong, leaving was the right thing to do, I was still only 23, young enough to start again. I just didn't know how to do it. I was scared.

It was on a Sunday evening, of the May bank holiday, in that year we had moved to our little bungalow with so much expectation put upon it, we went out to the town pub like so many times before. On this particular evening Andrew was horrible, he said I looked like a tart wearing leggings and made me change for jeans. His temper in the car was frightening. I was nervous all evening. I stood and looked at myself in the large mirror in the ladies for a while thinking what to do. I hugged him when I went back in, he pushed me off. I saw one of the other blokes take a second look as if he didn't quite see it right. Andrew was driving but still drank a fair amount. I was scared. He told me we were going, I defied him saying it was early, why leave. He grabbed my arm "Rosie now! I won't say it again" the landlady heard him and came over "everything alright you two? Little lovers tiff?" Christ little did she know. He glared at me as an unspoken warning not to reply.

I asked for another drink. Oh dear Rosie why did you ask for another drink. That gin and tonic barely touched the sides but all the time his hand touched my arm, his grip so tight it was hurting.

Now very rarely do I lose my temper, but when I do, I do. I whirled round to face him and in a slightly raised voice "No! I am not going home with you. I know what I'm going to get. I'm not having it anymore. You can fuck off". At that point I checked myself we were after all in a public place, and I was Rosie, fun and laughter Rosie. I jumped off my stool and left the pub. In hot pursuit of course, was Daphne! Followed by one of blokes we were friends with. I was thrown on to the car bonnet, he hit me hard then realised he had been watched, I thought he was going to get thumped as well. The guy grabbed him by the scruff of his neck, what was said I never heard and was never told. They came back to the car Andrew got in, the guy, lovely bloke he was, I always thought so, put his hands around my shoulders "go on love he'll not hurt you, just bit too much pop"

We drove home in silence, when we got near our turning, I asked him to take me straight to Mum's, of course he didn't, on the drive he tried to pull me out the car. I got out, but started to run as he put the key in the door, he grabbed me, soon over powered me, I kicked out at his face but, luckily, looking back on it, I missed, his rage was so fierce I do believe had my foot made contact with his face I may not have lived to tell the tale. I surrendered. He tore of my clothes, forced my legs apart and at that point I think I blacked out.

Next thing I knew there was light coming through the curtains, I was naked in bed, Andrew not there. Every single part of me hurt, I was heavily bruised, my inner thighs and arms the worst. I got out of bed, last night's clothes found quickly through the empty house. Just Rory and I there. I threw the basics in a bag. Put my dog on his lead and left.

I walked in tears into Mum's kitchen. Everything just spilled out of me. I felt every emotion it was possible to feel. Mum's MS tremoring hands tight around me and her words clear as though yesterday "oh my darling, that bastard will never ever hurt you again" Mum never swore.

Chapter 4

That first day back with Mum was strangely calm, we talked, I told her everything, she was devastated I had not told her sooner, but very comforting too. The money didn't matter one bit, she was happy to have Rory in the house and said I had complete freedom to come and go as I wished and could stay indefinitely.

On the Tuesday I went into work as normal. Within minutes of me sitting at my desk, the private line rang and it was him, I put the phone down. I went upstairs the Opticians examination room, he beckoned me in as he had five minutes before his first patient was due. I sat down and tried to find the words to tell him but I couldn't they wouldn't come, all that came was tears, floods and floods of tears. I didn't realise how much I had kept in to save my Mum more hurt. I took off my cardie and showed him the bruises, also the ones on my legs and he could see my cheek was swollen.

All I managed to actually say was his name. The Optician asked me two questions -

"Do you want me call the police?"

"Do you want to see him again?"

I just shook my head that was in my hands. I couldn't look at him. I felt guilty. I felt ashamed.

He rang downstairs for Becky to come up. Becky was the head receptionist and also who I was closest to at work.

They spoke, but I couldn't hear the words. Becky came over to me and took my hand gently "Rosie come on, let's go upstairs, some coffee, chocolate biscuits and hugs"

We did just that.

I talked to Becky for quite some time, I told her what had happened and bits of the past, most of that though I kept to myself, I hadn't told Mum all the details either. The guilt and shame I felt prevented me from letting the most hurtful details out. I just needed them to understand he had hurt me, so they could all help to keep him away from me. They all did.

That evening when I got home he turned up at the door, Mum sent away, he went. Later that evening he phoned, Mum told him to leave me alone and phone no more. The next morning some time before eight o'clock he came to the door, I answered it and just stared at him, his face all scratched, said he had crashed his car. I didn't believe this, he looked more like he'd had an argument with a rose bush. Looking at him, I felt no warmth or love for him whatsoever, I did however feel panic, my heart raced just at his presence. I closed the door and locked it. I never saw him again.

Everyone at work was amazing, so supportive, the Optician spoke to a solicitor friend of his and put the wheels in motion for me. Being with Mum again, just the two of us was exactly what I needed, no pressure, no expectation and most importantly no judgement. Night times however were difficult, I really can't explain why but I started having panic attacks, alone in my bed in the dark. Bloody scary too, the first time I thought I dying! I found it impossible to sleep, sporadic naps is the best way to describe it. I soon found however that with enough wine throughout the evening and I could pretty much knock myself out. I was expert at functioning with extreme efficiency with horrific hangovers. So life continued and I was for certain happy to finally be free.

For the first few weeks all I did was work and be at Mum's, furthest I ventured than that was the supermarket. I couldn't for the time being deal with more than that. Mum came with me to collect the rest of my things from the bungalow, clothes and personal possessions only, I was more than happy to leave all furniture and all other things, I wanted no reminders, the ones inside my head were going to be hard enough to cope with.

As the weeks went by I ventured out a little, to the town pub I used to love with Laura, the youngest of my work colleagues, nearest my age and a single girl we had fun together and became quite close. It was during these pub visits that I struck up a friendship with Gary Anderson. He lived in Rugby but drank there frequently as he worked in town. Gary was not at all good looking, he was married, although they were breaking up, but he was extremely intelligent with an infectious humour that I was attracted to.

Laura and I played pool with the guys in the pub and Gary was one of them. We started talking more and more, talking turned into flirting, built my confidence a little, certainly made me feel wanted.

It was on a night out with Laura that things happened between Gary and I, we went outside, to the back of the pub, as he was only recently separated from his wife he didn't want people to know, held my hand and pulled me close, holding both hands around my waist, I was nervous at first but his gentle grip relaxed me and we kissed passionately. Oh what a feeling it was, desire, I had forgotten it's power, I knew right there that this would not stop at one kiss!

Well, these occasions with Gary became more frequent; we even had days out together. Mum liked him and he came and stopped over after the three of us had a really great evening together.

The problem was however that Gary was a very big drinker, for him to sink five pints of lunchtime and then pour himself back into his works van was not unusual at all.

Most of these lunchtimes I would meet with him and although I only had a couple of drinks and was never late back for work, it didn't impress them much though, and quite rightly so, that I would return from lunch and greet patients on their arrival smelling like a drunk!

Felt torn with that because I didn't want to let Gary down but also work had been so wonderful about everything I really felt like I was taking the piss somewhat. Already by that time though for me to go into a public house and order a soft drink was simply unthinkable. I was without doubt by that time alcohol dependant and feelings of guilt for that were prominent.

While working at the Opticians when you worked at Saturday morning you were given a half day off in the week. On one of these half days I went home to Mum's at lunchtime, glorious sunny day, Mum and I ate lunch in the garden with a bottle of wine, the bottle quite easily turned into two. The phone rang, it was Gary, he had a job out in the country and wondered if I would like to meet him at pub there for a couple. Of course I would do this, at that time, drink driving was illegal but a thing still quite commonly done. It was lovely country pub with my favourite cider on tap, we sat outside and chatted our way through three pints each.

On the way home there was an incident where a small boy on a bike had his back wheel clipped by a car, as he and his friends decided to run the traffic. As witnesses we stayed at the scene until the police arrived. The driver was not to blame, that was quickly established. The police however decided to breath test the driver and the witnesses. As the policeman approached me, breathalyser in hand, my heart sank, he was not suspicious at all about my alcohol consumption in the slightest, I had an immense tolerance to booze from many years of drinking in great quantities. He explained it was simply routine and didn't expect a problem. He passed me the breathalyser, I did my worst, and there it was, a massive high reading. The officer was lovely and suspected that there was a problem with the unit. I told him I had drank a couple of ciders, being economical with the truth, I omitted the details of the wine. He took me to the station were once again my reading was extremely high, they were so kind to me though, they let me use the phone to call Mum so she wasn't worried and advised me to ask for a blood test which I did.

Waiting for the Doctor to arrive at the station to perform the test, they gave me orange juice to drink and left me alone in a room after suggesting I might like to do a few exercises. I ran around that small room for nearly an hour until the Doctor finally came. After the blood test, I was free to go, after receiving my charge for drinking under the influence of alcohol, court case pending.

I was just so cross with myself, I deserved to lose my licence, I had broken the law plain and simple, poor Mum however did not need the extra stress and knowing that following the court case I would lose my licence and she would lose her only method of transport, I food shopped for her, took her to appointments when necessary and after all she had done for me I had abused her trust for nothing other than my own selfishness! I was mortified, and rightly so.

The Court appearance soon came round, Gary took me, knowing that my licence would be revoked and would be unable to drive home.

I was given a short time with the duty solicitor prior to my hearing, I was very lucky. He was understanding and sympathetic, saying that given the seriousness of my Mother's condition, the recent turmoil that had occurred in my own life, we should be able to get the best result possible in the situation.

I received a fairly hefty fine but only the mandatory twelve months ban, no extra. With that result I had to be relieved, as the outcome could have been very much worse.

We walked from the Court room, with my driving licence no longer in my possession because of my ridiculously heavy drinking habit. I asked Gary to take me straight to the pub!

Looking back at this point in my life I can see that my behaviour was inexcusable. There were two reasons for that, firstly, with so much pain living in my head and my heart, I found solace at the end of a bottle. Secondly, in your twenties you feel invincible.

Also there was the fact that due to previous events in my life my image of myself was pretty poor, confidence invisible. I thought I had to be the way people wanted me to be for them to like me. So as for Gary, a heavy drinker and social animal, I thought I needed to be the same for him to want me. Difference being, when the evening was finished he would happily drink coffee and go to bed, where as I would get back to Mum's, open yet another bottle of wine, and sit, usually alone, and weep.

I managed relatively well without a car. Gary picked me up from Mum's of a morning in order for me to be at work in good time. Then of an evening one of the Opticians would take me home, as he passed the village on his way home. Rory was fine of a lunchtime, now that bit older and of course being with Mum all day, he was in and out of the garden as he wished and had company too. Mum adored having him there with her, they soon became very best friends. Rory had pretty much become Mum's dog, which suited us both.

Food shop was sorted by Gary and I one week, then Tom the next week.

Mum and I still were very close, spending a great deal of time together, either just the two of us or with Gary also.

Although things had levelled out somewhat, I was still having panic attacks at night time. I had visited my Doctor and was referred to a lovely lady for counselling. It was during my visits to her that I, for the first time, talked about my drinking. Of course she agreed that my consumption was well above what it should be, more important she felt was the reasons why I drank to such excess. I could not talk about, my father, the abuse within my marriage or my feelings towards myself. So this lady was immensely helpful in giving advice in the management of my panic attacks, the practical help. Deeper hurt I had to leave where it was. Too painful to dig up again. I finished my counselling with her within only a few weeks. Leaving the roots to all my evils well and truly buried, hidden within me like a burning flame I could not put out.

As the end of the year approached I started to feel that I needed to find some independence. Whilst living with Mum was wonderful, I felt I was relying too much on other people. I needed to put some strength back into myself. I began to look at small flats to rent in the town where I worked. Walking to and from work then would be easy and no more asking for lifts. My wage was not a great one, so I was very limited on what I could afford, I found a one up one down property with its own drive and a little garden. Partially furnished and just in budget, it was perfect and I actually really liked it too.

Telling Mum I was moving was not easy. With no transport it would mean that for the remaining months of my ban I would see much less of Mum. She totally understood my reasons though and was, as always completely supportive. We came to the mutual decision that Rory would remain with her. This softened the blow of my departure and eased my mind as to Mum's loneliness. Her multiple sclerosis was quite active too and this remained great concern for us both.

Early December of that year I got the keys to number 122, my own little place, for the first time, somewhere that was utterly and totally mine.

The decree nisi of my divorce also came through. As I divorced him on the grounds of unreasonable behaviour and he did not contest, the whole process was a formality. One of little emotion for myself and every step took me further away from the memories of that time, with that the happier I became.

My little 122 was my haven. With photographs and pictures soon in place. Bedding and towels from home and some souvenirs I still had from my holidays with Mum, this little place quickly was my home sweet home.

There is however always a downside, not seeing as much of Mum was the main one, but also the close proximity that I now was from the pub, that pub, the town pub I did really like.

Luckily though my tight budget prevented visits to the establishment as regularly as I would have quite liked.

Quite often on a Saturday afternoon however, that pub became my destination, one of the lads I was, Gary even described me as a chap with tits! This reputation I was more than happy with.

These times were good. Everything going from strength to strength at work. I had my own little den, my little 122. Time spent with Mum although less frequent was precious. I helped her all I could. Gary and I were just having fun. Work hard. Play hard. Happy times.

Christmas of that year I spent the whole day with my Mum. Christmas eve was of course spent in the pub for the entire day and night. Gary had stayed with me so he dropped me at Mum's on the way to his.

It was lovely Christmas Day, just my Mum, my Nan and me.

Thomas was with his in laws.

The three of us had a full Christmas lunch that I cooked, myself. Rory lay happily under the table.

Then Nan went home, as other relatives visited her for Christmas tea. Mum and I drank wine and boozy coffee eating chocolates and watching Christmas television, for the rest of the day.

I slept in my own room, with no panic attacks. Most of Boxing day I also spent with Mum too. It was quite simply a beautiful Christmas full of fond memories.

New Year's Eve is always a massive one in the drinking calendar! This year for Gary and I was certainly no exception. We spent the evening in an older pub in town with two very good friends. Live band playing and the place was packed, the atmosphere was electric. Having never spent a New Year's Eve out before I loved every minute of it. Dancing to the band, everyone was happy, chatting to people, some I hadn't seen from school. It was a wicked night, and yes I drank a lot but no more than anybody else.

As the night drew to a close, Auld Lang Syne was sung, toasts were made and hugs and kisses for dear ones and strangers alike.

Gary arranged for us to go home with our friends to continue the celebrations at their house. I really was tired enough to go straight home, also aware of the fact that I had drank plenty already.

The four of us started the walk to their house, despite my pleas to go directly home. We reached a junction, where one path would take us to their house and in the other direction was my safe little 122.

I stood for a moment "Rosie for fuck sake come on" Gary sniped. This was a new way for him to speak to me, a new way I didn't like!

I called to our friends who were a little further ahead by this time " I'm gonna head off home guys, great night, see you soon" They replied and we exchanged a few more words and laughter. I started off home with Gary but he was in a bad temper. My heart raced with that familiar feeling and alarm bells in my head. I turned to face Gary, within a second, both his hands were on my shoulders and with full force he pushed me flat on the grass. In one swift action he pulled me up by my hair "get up you pathetic bitch" I was numb, completely numb.

Again? Seriously? Happy fucking New Year Rosie!

Chapter 5

After the New Year's Eve incident Gary was genuinely sorry, I felt for him because I could see remorse and sorrow in his eyes, something that was never there following any situation of that nature in my marriage. Gary explained that New Year's Eve was always a hard time for him as a child. Both his parents were big drinkers and not adverse to violence when inebriated. I knew this, we had spoken about it before, and because it, I thought, I hoped for it to be an isolated incident. Our relationship continued.

However, my confidence was shaken again and I started questioning the events of New Year, because all be there good were reasons for his actions, it was still violence, the one thing I had run away from. Arguments started to creep in over trivial things. I needed some space, I had to be strong, so I asked him to stay away for a while, he kicked off but went after a few choice words.

My Father's birthday was the 17th of March, I remember the first anniversary of his birthday when I was fourteen, after school before Mum returned from work, in my room, listening to one of his albums, Simon and Garfunkel, I cried so hard I lost control and took a compass to my wrist. Stabbing it as hard as I could into my skin. I didn't really do much damage when I cleaned it up, popped a plaster on, pulled my jumper sleeve down and went downstairs to cook dinner for Mum and Tom on their return from work.

On that year, living on my own Daddy's birthday was as painful then as it was every year, if not more so, I was alone, Mum becoming more disabled by her condition almost daily. Knowing how upset I was going to be, Tom agreed to have Mum with him for dinner on that day.

I was free to drink. Making sure there was wine in the fridge for later, I took myself off to the pub. More than comfortable drinking alone, I sat at the bar with my pint, and the many that followed, taking in the random conversation around me and drifting into my own space periodically.

Plenty I drank that day, feeling my mood starting to drop and fighting tears, as painful memories spiked my heart. I decided to head off home.

As much as I loved my little 122, on that day every part of everything made me feel loss, bereavement, and resentment I once again lost control. Precious souvenirs, pictures, a vase bought for me from Kate, were all hurled at the wall. I screamed, I smashed, I broke everything I could put my hand to. With every possession I held dear to me in bits, I collapsed to the floor. The most broken of all was me!

The morning after an episode such as that one is always a sobering affair. The realisation that no matter how much alcohol is consumed, the pain still remains, and is waiting, magnified to greet you! Only now accompanied by a smack in the face hangover and the devastation created by blind stupidity, the result of a destructive cocktail of booze and deep lost emotion.

Thomas picked me up and took me to Mum's for the remainder of that weekend. Completely oblivious to the pain I carried around inside me, Thomas knew some of the details to my marriage breakdown, he knew there had been violence but as with Mum, I kept the worst of it to myself. Worried by what Tom may do, had he known the full extent of what I had been through. I was after all his little sister and he had a temper of his own that could easily have resulted in him being responsible for serious damage to the apology of a man I married.

On my way home from work one evening, I called into the pub, fully intending to just have one drink and go home. When I walked in, the first face I say was Gary's. With his works van parked around the back, I didn't know he was there, had I of known I would not have gone. I went to my normal spot at the bar, it was pretty empty at that time in the evening, thinking to myself "one drink Rosie, down it quick and be off".

Before I could finish my pint Gary came over. Telling me how much he had missed me and could he buy me a drink. I agreed and we talked. Intelligent, witty man Gary was and all those things were still there.

Soon two pints turned into many pints which resulted in Gary coming home with me.

The following morning we both had work but arranged to meet up later.

Gary and I decided to give us another try. This time he was going to move into my little 122, I was unsure about that part but we did it anyway. The first few weeks were great. We actually both drank less, spending more time just together rather than out at the pub. With Gary back to help me with transport I was able to see more of Mum and my Nan, I missed them both terribly.

I still had that little doubt in my mind that never left me though after New Year's Eve.

With the two of us living together it soon became evident that my little 122 simply was not big enough. With our wages combined, we could afford somewhere bigger. We found a nice one bed roomed flat in an old building in the centre of town. Much larger living area and a proper sized bedroom. Our lodge flat was our new home.

I hoped this fresh start, for us both would be a happy one.

One weekend, just for the Sunday, Gary and I went to Shropshire for the day, took Rory too, with a walk down the Long Mynd planned. The day started really well, but Rory was not really what you could call a well-trained dog, the opposite in fact. Poor dog had never had anyone take the time with him that any young puppy needs. He was well loved and cared for, but obedient? No!

This irritated Gary one hell of a lot, he was a cat man, not a dog man so an ill-mannered black lab wasn't easy for him to tolerate.

The entire walk, he swore, moaned, shouted and swore some more! I just kept my head down, thinking of the pub grub at the end and thinking to myself "this is not the man I want to share my life with"

The very day after our day trip to Shropshire, I was at work as normal, when I had a phone call; Mum had fallen badly at home and was being taken to Northampton General Hospital. I got hold of Gary and he was able to take time out to just drop me at the hospital.

My dear Mum, in a hospital bed, she was always such a strength, independent despite her condition, but here she looked so venerable and so bereft, every little tiny little piece of me went out to her.

I quickly got the run down from the nurse, it seemed nothing was broken, she was just badly shaken and her MS had gone into a flare up due to the fall.

Having established the facts, I placed myself down next to Mum's bed, held her hand tight, reassured her in every way possible, that very soon she would be well, back at home, with Rory and I would be making us both and Nan, a lovely roast dinner.

This was not the case at all.

After just over a week Mum was discharged to a small hospital in the local town. She was relieved, we both were, that at least she was closer to home. It would be much easier for Tom to visit and within walking distance for me. We all hoped however that this too would be only for a short time.

Once again our hopes were not reality.

Mum's condition showed no signs of improvement. Weeks ticked by, and although she had regular visitors, the staff were all wonderful and she was well looked after, the majority of the patients were years older than my Mum and she desperately missed her home, Rory was constantly on her mind. We could not see an end in sight, she had improved to point and then remained there.

Thomas and I were asked to attend a meeting, with the doctors and nursing staff involved with Mum's care.

We were told, that from what they could see, Mum's mobility was unlikely to improve. It was diagnosed that Mum had progressed from Relapsing Remitting Multiple Sclerosis to Secondary Progressive MS.

With this fact in mind they had to recommend that she was unable to return home without full time care.

A care package was to be put in place that consisted of two full time carers to live in and provide twenty four hour care on a rotation basis, initially for a week at a time each.

I asked if I could be one of the carers, being more than willing to give up my job. This could not be the case. As a relation, the regulations of the care package stated that I could not be paid for any care I gave. I found this utterly ridiculous. They would happily pay a complete stranger, but as Mum's daughter, even if I took the required training, I could not receive a wage.

So the decision was made.

It took time to find the right carers. Tom and I set up my old bedroom as a private room for the live in lady, whom ever she may be. We put in a portable television, and an arm chair, it was already nicely decorated, so the room was ready.

I visited Mum, excited to tell her about the room and how the house was spotless and all ready for her return.

One of the nurses caught me before I got to the main day room where I knew Mum would be. "Rosie, just quickly before you see Jean, she has had a difficult day and is quite upset"

I didn't say a word to Mum I just hugged her tight, she talked about the situation she now found herself in, how she felt she had lost her womanhood. With Multiple Sclerosis when it becomes progressive, once you lose control of a part of your body you rarely get it back.

That was the day my dearest Mother had her catheter fitted.

Chapter 6

Whilst Mum was still waiting for the carers to be put in place, I was in the village walking Rory one day, when I saw the old gentleman who did some gardening work for my Mum and lived opposite my Nan, he said Nan had asked would I pop in after walking Rory. I thought this strange only because I would have done so anyway and also for my dear Nan to ask for anything was unheard of.

When I walked into Nan's old cottage, summer but it was still cold. She was sat on a chair in a really strange position and was as white as a ghost, " it's alright duck don't worry" she said quite clearly in bloody agony "I fell down putting the washing out this morning and I think I've done something" Bless her heart, it was obvious something was badly wrong. I ran as quickly as I could round the corner to the phone box and dialled 999.

Waiting with her for the ambulance to arrive, she explained how she had dragged herself from the garden into the cottage. She had been sitting on that chair for hours!

As soon as the ambulance pulled up, opposite the green, the closest point that a vehicle could get to Nan's cottage without driving across the village green, which quite frankly I expected them to do. I rushed over to them, explained to them what had happened and that my Nan, who normally was extremely fit for a lady of her years, was unable to walk, they would need a stretcher, or to bring the ambulance closer. They explained how they were used to handling elderly ladies and they would support her. I protested that she was not capable of walking. They knew old ladies but they did not know my Nan, I did!

They believed because she fell in the garden and was able to get herself back into the house that it was nothing too serious.

They stood one either side of her, supporting her from under her arms, I could see the agony in her face as they proceeded to walk her across the green. I was livid and screaming at them, they still didn't listen and it did it their way.

Once at the hospital, I helped Nan into a hospital gown, she never complained about anything and she still didn't on this day. Once seen by the doctor and then the x ray confirmed she had badly broken her pelvis. She was to remain lying down for three weeks and would be cared for there at St. Cross Hospital in Rugby for the duration.

So now I had one of the people I loved most in the world in one Hospital in one town and the other in another Hospital in another town. Thank fuck I thought that I was counting down the days to when very shortly I would have my driving licence back.

Later that evening, I had the awful job of having to tell Mum about Nan's fall, explain about the hospital and the length of her stay knowing how distraught Mum would be that she couldn't get herself to go and visit her own mother. I was right, she was very upset, I calmed her with the knowledge that the very last thing Nan would want was for her to be upset. Nan's last words to me that day were "give my love to Jean".

Such a difficult week I had ahead of me until I got my licence back. Mum within walking distance still from our lodge flat but Nan a good twenty minute drive. I wanted to see them both every day. Be there for them both. It was tough. I took a week's holiday off from work so I could visit them both at times when people could take me and able to use public transport at other times.

The day I got my licence back was a very good day. I visited my loved ones. Took all their washing with me, cleaned and dried it, and then visited them again!

That evening Gary was out and I sat listening to music in the flat with a big fat bottle of wine, back in the day when you could buy a big fat bottle of wine!

There were still a million holes in my relationship with Gary. For the time being though I had so much to deal with, I could not give it much headspace.

Always there though, eating silently away at me, the thought that I was taking myself down a familiar road and I should turn back before I go too far. I shed a lot of tears that night on my own, tears for Daddy, I missed him so much, he was a wise man my father, always knew exactly what to say in every situation, never raised his voice, gave us nothing but love and knowledge, I always had something to learn from him, he only had a short time to tell me the things he would want to tell me throughout my life, he did his best to make me strong, hoping to leave me well equipped for life. I knew that's what he was doing. I loved that man with all my heart, nothing and nobody could ever replace him. I reached for more wine.

Finally, suitable carers to meet Mum's needs were found. Tom and I were to get to meet them first.

We had already sorted not only their room, but once again converted the dining room in Mum's house into a bedroom. The same as it had been for Daddy years before, even with the same bed, the very bed where Daddy lost his fight.

The first two cares were lovely, Elouise was in her twenties, only a little younger than me and had worked in the caring profession all of her working life. Angela was a lot younger and this was her first job of this nature, this worried me but she was a lovely girl and I was well prepared to help them both settle in, and get to know Mum.

This whole process was extremely hard for Mum, yes of course she was desperate to come home, but her home had been changing during her absence, she would have complete strangers initially, looking after her and also using her home as if it were their own.

My Mum was massively independent. She was also a very house proud woman with almost unrealistically high standards, even her own Mother didn't wash up to Mum's liking!

Thrifty too my Mum, she saved energy where ever possible, the oven only went on twice a week, not a spec of food was ever wasted, in her better days on a Sunday when she was at home all of the day she would make herself a flask of coffee to save repeatedly boiling the kettle and was often ironing at stupid o'clock when the electricity was on cheap rate, two jumpers went on before the heating.

I was a tad concerned that these lovely girls would have their work cut out with my Mum.

Mum was bought home in an ambulance, in the wheelchair that was now her legs. Rory was beside himself with excitement, I too was there waiting for her. We had some time on our own before the care manager drove to the village with Elouise. It was a good thing I thought that as the girl with the most experience she should do the first week.

I had tried to prepare Mum, not only for her own feelings but to also be aware of how difficult this would be for the girls too. Neither of them had taken a residential post such as this one and being away from loved ones for a week would not be easy for them.

When Elouise arrived, we did all the necessary introductions, then the care manager left us. The three of sat and talked for a while, Mum was also to have a district nurse come in daily to attend to her medical needs and help the carers to wash and change her.

I could tell Mum liked Elouise, pretty easy to read my Mother and had she not liked her it would have been blatantly obvious.

I showed Elouise everything she needed to know, she admitted she was not a great cook, mental note made to add a few ready meals to the shopping list!

When I sure it was the right time, I left them alone. Although emotional to accept this new way of life for my Mum who had already suffered more than one person should have to, it was also an incredible relief to leave her knowing she was safe at home and going to be well cared for.

I could not remember the last time I had left Mum's house without great concern that she may come to harm. I smiled. Driving straight to St Cross to see Nan and tell her all the news.

Nan was making fantastic process, for a woman of her age, her brake was healing well. She was a dream to look after, being grateful for everything she was given.

She had other family members visiting her too and she was quite a solitary character anyway, didn't need company, much like myself, solitude is essential.

Telling her of Mum's new home set up, how lovely the girl was and how Mum seemed to warm to her, I could tell it was mixed emotions for her as myself, relief on one hand sadness on the other.

Very soon Nan was heading home too although neither of her sons had done anything to make her home habitable. How two fit healthy adult men both in the building trade could think it acceptable for their own Mother to live in a cottage with no central heating or bathroom was completely beyond me and angered me somewhat to say the least. Nan however didn't mind at all and was just glad to be going home.

Mum settled into her new life with life relatively easily, although it was evidence almost immediately that her firm favourite was Elouise. This made life very difficult for poor Angela, who really was a lovely girl, but she was fighting a losing battle trying to win the affection of a stubborn lady who favoured someone else. I did what I could to ease the situation, making my visits more frequent when Angela was there. I talked with her a lot, apologising for Mum's lack of warmth towards her, trying to help her and Mum to build a bond as best I could.

Constantly I was battling myself for Gary's love and understanding which I badly needed at this time. He was never resentful or controlling over the amount of time I needed to spend in the village, the opposite in fact, he was supportive in that way. His feelings towards me though I was never sure of, he angered quickly when drunk, verbally aimed directly at me.

Gary had taken voluntary redundancy from his job and was working as a taxi driver to fill in until he made a decision as to what he did next.

This did mean that we had less disposable income than before.

At this time too Gary was in the process of selling his

marital home and going through a divorce, this all lead to him spending a certain amount of time talking with his almost ex-wife on the phone and I found myself feeling that I was being compared to her, this was in no way helping my already seriously dented confidence.

With everything going on in my life at that time, although Gary was far from perfect, I did not want to have to face things alone.

So one Friday night I planned to make it a sexy night, he wasn't working so as soon as got back to the flat I had a long bath making sure I was ready, he dived in the bath after me, so I had time dress in sexy underwear, best perfume on and then I waited for him on the bed.

He came from the bathroom, towel round his waste to find me sexily clad in my best 'come to bed pose' with eyes to match.

Gary looked me up and down, and without a change to the expression on his face or to the contents of his towel, icily said "do you think you laying there star shaped is going to get me going" He turned away and started dressing.

Mortified I was, cold as ice he was.

"Get dressed then, I want to get to the pub!"

Chapter 7

Family life for my loved ones in the village was as settled as it could be. Problems were ongoing with Mum's twenty four hour care, I felt very tied by my full time job and unable to help more. On the whole though, the system did work.

Nan was amazing, back up to full strength physically but showing some worrying signs in her behaviour. Again making me wish I could be there for her more.

One Sunday, just the two of us Gary and I took off to The Malvern Hills for the day to discuss our future. Walking gear on, always something Gary and I had both enjoyed, this time just us, we parked up and took off for the hills, complete with picnic and 4 pack.

It was a fine day, not sunny, just pleasantly warm, perfect for walking and photography.

We walked for an hour or so then found a small secluded place to sit. There on that day, we discussed everything, my concerns over our relationship, my fear of the future for my Mum and my Nan and the possibility of me looking for a different job to give me more time.

All afternoon we sat there. Until my bladder stated enough was enough. We had decided that, I would resign from the Opticians, we would pull our recourses and set up a mobile catering business, basically a burger van! Just more up market.

We both caught the sun on that day, along with a direction that had previously been missing.

Wasting no time, we spent every spare minute either researching where we would be able pitch our van, food stuffs we could serve or looking for a suitable van. We both took the basic food hygiene course. I handed in my notice at work. We both became thoroughly engrossed in our new venture.

Once we were both agreed on a suitable van, we decided upon The Hungry Toad as its name, to be sign written on the side. Membership to the local Cash and Carry stores sorted and business bank account along with an accountant to guide us through, we were all set.

The first place we took our van was to the outside of Mum's house! We pitched up, heated the griddle, fired up the urn and made dinner for Mum and anyone else who went past right there in her residential street. The street I lived on as a child, it was perfect. Obviously more for Mum than anything, but a good little trial run.

Once the toad was up and running we settled well into working together in such close proximity, the logistics though of having a catering trailer parked in your one allocated parking space of the lodge flat block, quite some distance from the flat itself which was also on the second floor, proved problematic!

Large water containers, cool boxes of food and bags of

varies types of bread, and other food stuffs had to be loaded every morning. Storing all this in our one bed roomed flat also a great problem.

Search began for another property to rent with more space inside and its own drive.

I took a couple of extra jobs on too, serving in local bars, this was fine because we packed up the trailer around two o'clock in the afternoon, that left Gary free to go for any required stock and me to go to the village and spend a couple of hours with Mum and Nan, before work in the bar started. So although hectic and tiring, it did work, we just needed a new place to live that would accommodate us both and The Toad.

There was however more violence, after one night out, when I had done something wrong, what exactly escapes me but Gary pushed me into the empty bath at the flat.

Christmas eve he locked me out after a night out and I had to call the police to get them to break in.

Gary had to brothers and on separate occasions they both addressed him for his treatment of me. Gary was the eldest though and was not affected at all by their opinions telling them both in no uncertain terms to fuck off!

Although Gary had these outbursts, they were only when he was well inebriated. The rest of the time he was supportive over issues with my family. We worked well together. So I accepted his flaws as just part of him and I could live with them, for the time being at least.

We found ourselves a pleasant enough 3 bed semi in a decent part of town, with a drive large enough for our car and also the trailer. It was a good sized corner plot. One bedroom we planned to use simply as a stock room with a large freezer and extra fridge that would make our lives much easier. The property itself wasn't well looked after and we agreed with the owner that if we replaced the kitchen and decorated throughout he would carpet all the way through and give us the first month rent free.

Running The Toad, doing 2 bar jobs, all shopping for Mum and Nan and varies other things for them along with constant decorating was not easy. We were both exhausted and fractious.

Once our new home No 19 was all finished things settled down somewhat. The Catering business was successful on a daily basis, we had a regular spot on one of the industrial estates in town. On top of this we did some weekend work at local dog shows, fetes and open days. The wage from this though, with the higher rent for our new home, was barely enough for us both and we wanted to do more trips away.

Camping and walking on our free weekends was something we both enjoyed.

I could however, easily run the trailer on my own and was actually quite keen to do so, put some distance between us and give me some thinking space. So Gary commenced his search for alternative employment.

I was very worried about my Nan at this point, she seemed paler every time I saw her and just not herself.

She would say some very alarming things. Blackened saucepans I found one day and her neighbour also expressed his concerns, reporting having seen Nan putting her washing out both extremely early in the morning and in the rain!

This was all of course, cause for great concern. I did have a conversation with my uncle about it, my Mum's eldest brother, the only one who, except for me visited Nan on a regular basis. He dismissed it saying she was just getting on in years, which of course she was, but it worried me terribly that she may come to some harm on her own with her only heating one electric fire and an open fire!

I worried too that she wasn't eating properly, I bought her shopping every week but meat she would buy for herself from the butchers and I cooked for her and Mum usually once a week, I was still concerned.

At home my alcohol consumption had gone soaring through the roof! Both my bar jobs allowed free drink whilst working, they were rough pubs, not the sort that many girls would want to work in, but having been a big drinker in the town for a long time, I was not intimidated in the slightest by the clientele, the opposite in fact, I got on well with most of them and they looked out for me. Gary had to be careful how he spoke to me in these pubs and had I told one of a number of these gents what Gary was capable of doing to me when pissed up, he would have taken a serious beating, without a doubt.

There was by this time so many things tying us together,

it would have been hard for me to leave. We did have good times too, very good times, which outweighed his occasional drunken dangerous behaviour. I convinced myself of this anyway.

The incidents did not increase in frequency but they did in severity. On one occasion after a particularly raucous night out we rowed when we got home because I wanted another drink, Gary said I had already had too much, he was right, but I had one anyway, so the argument continued into the bedroom where I stumbled and fell onto the floor, on my side, right next to the bed, he stamped on my head breaking both my ear rings. That was by far the worst thing he had done up to that point and it left me devastated. I drove to Mum's the next day and spent the day there. Nan came round too. I took Rory for a long walk along the canal, walking is always good for thinking, right up to the point where the silly sod fell in, big black labs make quite a splash when they hit the cut, which he did, all over a nicely dressed couple having a relaxing Sunday stroll!

One of my Sundays at work, as was quite usual the Rugby lads came in following their game. Normal crowd, just myself and the boss behind the bar, that was quite normal too, it was only a small place, desirable to only a certain crowd of rough!

On this day they were very rowdy, and it was busy, I went out from behind the bar to clear glasses and do the ashtrays, I turned round quickly and without even seeing it an ice cube hit me smack, right in the centre of my eye. I put my hand on it, it was mighty painful, I grabbed

Gary's arm "something just hit me in the eye, it feels bad" I was nearly crying with pain, his eyes never left his pint "fuck off Rosie, get back to work"

I went to the ladies and looked in the mirror, as I stood there I quite literally watched my eyeball fill with blood. Oh shit I thought, having worked in an Opticians for over five years I knew that this could be something serious. I had no intention of asking Gary to come with me but I knew I had to go to eye casualty. I told my boos, he saw my eye and was quite alarmed even in his pissed up state and phoned Phil, a taxi driver who had a massive soft spot for me, had rescued me from many a drunken scrape. Sunday evening so he wasn't busy and came immediately to pick me up.

When we got to Northampton General Hospital Phil would not hear of me giving him any money, he also would not hear of leaving me alone and waited with me until I was seen.

Thankfully I did not have a detached retina because that would have required urgent surgery in Oxford! They put a patch over my eye and said I must return in the morning when the swelling and blood had cleared so they could take another look. Phil took me home. Gary was in bed.

I poured myself a drink and sat on the back door step, despite the steroid drops, my eye was still painful, I tried not to cry, looking at the stars begging my Dad for help, as I had done before, oh Rosie I thought, why are you so stupid that men just want to hurt you. I couldn't answer my question.

In the morning, when Gary saw my eye and my tears, he looked horrified, "why the hell didn't you tell me it was that bad?" I wiped away my own tears "you weren't exactly in a listening mood!"

Gary took me back to the hospital, they gave me more drops and said no heavy lifting as such a trauma to the eye would leave it venerable for some time and a visit to my Opticians would also be necessary in a few weeks.

As we drove home Gary put his hand over onto my knee "I am really sorry Rosie, I was a prick not to listen to you last night, sorry".

One lovely thing we did was go on a short four night break to a hotel in Jersey. The place that held so many beautiful memories for me, ones I wanted to replace, temporarily distorted by my honeymoon.

I chose a hotel in a location the opposite end of the island to where I stayed with him. I knew Gary would appreciate the gorgeous view over Mont Orgueil Castle and the village of Gorey itself had a nice selection of restaurants and bars. With good walking all around I was confident he would approve.

We took the car so we could tour and take plenty of luggage, which included all our walking gear and cameras and accessories. We really did have a wonderful four days making the most of every moment. Gary took me to all the places I wanted to visit. We sat waiting for the perfect sunset photo. We ate Italian. We walked the paths I remembered. He left me to think for a while at different times.

My warmth for the Island returned, I laughed out loud when I remembered the spot where a seagull had done his worst all over Tom. Overwhelmed by the feeling of pride that pricked my memory of sitting on Daddy's lap in his wheelchair and the day I pushed him myself, shopping in St. Helier for presents for Mum. We even drove past the hotel we stayed at in St Ouen and drove the length of the bay stopping to take photographs as often as I wished, something he had never let me do or caused a fuss when I asked. We had the perfect time, had I have known however that it would be the last time I was to visit this beautiful Island, that filled my heart with love and laughter, I would have given it an extra special goodbye.

Chapter 8

There had been a few changes with Mum's care package. The girls had found a week at a time too much to be away from their homes, so it was adjusted to a four day turn around.

Poor Angela had had to leave, she tried her very best to win Mum's confidence, but because Mum had a strong bond with Elouise, Angela was second best and the girl was too young to handle the obvious difference in feelings Mum had for them.

We had quite a number of different carers come and go. It sure wasn't an easy job, they did however get paid extremely well.

Mum's MS was worsening all the time, but she never lost her sense of humour, taking every new challenge with amazing strength. This wasn't helped by certain carers though, who did the bare minimum as far as nutrition was concerned and were not adverse to allowing Mum her favourite tipple of Gin and bitter lemon from lunchtime onwards.

My mother had always loved a drink, it was from her I learned my trade! Given the opportunity she would drink all day and the argument was always there, that, really, what else did she have.

With carers who did readily ply her with booze without a thought, either out of pity for her, or for their own gain, because immobile pissed up Jean would eventually fall asleep for a few hours, giving them free time.

This made Elouise's job so much harder on her return, she genuinely cared for Mum and they had become close, but alcohol is a powerful demon when used inappropriately and to excess.

Elouise was a very special girl, giving her utmost love and attention to Mum at all times and also had a wonderful way of turning an unpleasant situation around.

On one of my normal visits, I went through the back door into the kitchen as normal, the door into the dining room that was Mum's room was closed, it was only ever closed when things of a personal nature were being attended to. I could hear giggles, I called hello ... "oh Rosie, we are in a bit of a mess here aren't we Jean" Mum was laughing so hard she couldn't reply ... "we've got shit everywhere haven't we Jean" Mum still laughing "We won't be long Rosie, your Mum and I have just got to clean ourselves up" Mum still laughing.

The girl was an angel.

It was a very sad day, when Elouise decided she had to leave.

When she first came to Mum, she was quite recently married, the time her husband and her were away from each other was starting to come between them and she simply had to put him first. On her last day I went over with flowers and gifts. I cried. Elouise cried. I began to think poor Mum would never stop crying.

They did find however a very good replacement for Elouise.

Laura, was a lot older and again a very experienced carer. She took no nonsense from Mum, curbing her drinking somewhat and putting in the effort to get to know Mum properly. She asked to see photos of Daddy and talked with Mum a lot about him, Mum's life and Tom and me. She took Rory on long walks when Mum had visitors, which was a nice touch.

So, although Elousie's departure had been a painful one, Laura had brought with her a new set of qualities and was also a very good cook!

The young girl she shared the job with however was the opposite and the most thoughtless and unreliable to date. These two carers shared the post for some time.

The carers had the job of keeping the house clean and tidy. We had a gardener so they were not responsible for that. They also were not permitted to clean or have any cause to go into Mum's old bedroom upstairs. The double bed was made and her dressing table as she left it. I myself went in there regularly to dust and hoover. This was Mum's only request when the carers came to her home, was for me only to clean her precious things and for her room to remain as it was.

All the carers were made aware of this when they started and shown the air cupboard where all Mum's clothes were kept. Therefore they had no reason what so ever to enter that room.

On one of my normal visits, Laura was there having just started her days on, I went upstairs after chatting with them both for a while, the door to Mum's room was slightly open so I knew straight away someone had been in there, as I always left it completely closed.

I went over to her dressing table, everything looked the same, but when I opened her jewellery box it was empty. I gaped at the box in total dismay, how cruel was that, to steal the worthless jewellery of the very disabled lady you are there to care for, while she is sitting below unaware that the priceless memories of her late husband are being taken.

I sat on the bed sobbed. How was I going to tell her this? I needed to gather my thoughts and pull myself together!

When I got downstairs I called Laura into the kitchen, I told her first, watching closely the expressions on her face, her reactions to the news. I considered myself a relatively good judge of character, despite my disastrous choice of men, and the lady stood in front of me was not the thief, she looked as distraught as I felt whispering, with tears in her eyes "oh God Rosie how are we going to tell Jean" I held her hand "the best way we can, come on".

My Mum was jovial when we went back into the living room "what are you two planning" she said smiling. We both sat down on either side of her. The news visibly left her bereft, "my engagement ring? My wedding ring?"

she struggled even to get the words out. Poor Mum's fingers had swollen with inactivity so she could no longer wear them.

The three of sat and sobbed, it was just beyond comprehension. The jewellery was of very little value, yet priceless to the lady it was taken from. Still words escape me where this event is concerned.

We knew of course who it must have been, and by the time I got home my distress was quelled by anger. I went straight to the telephone to call the care manager, the conversation was not pretty, he was adamant that none of his employees were capable of such atrocity. I had no proof but to me it was black and white, there was one culprit and one only. He refused to take responsibility and even question the girl, conveniently she had resigned, and he had no forwarding address.

That was it, no more could be done.

I phoned Mum with the news, how much more did my beautiful darling Mum have to go through, life was too cruel to her. Too cruel to me. I opened a bottle of wine. Then another.

Over the following days, when possible I trailed round any of the jewellers that bought second hand stock, in both the local small town and the further a field in Rugby and Northampton, it was a fruitless search, Gary mocked me for even trying and I didn't tell Mum, so not to build her hopes up.

I never found them. Questioning how on earth some

people sleep at night.

Only a few weeks after the jewellery episode, when thankfully once again Laura was with Mum, I got an early morning call from the lovely lady, beside herself, having to tell me that an ambulance was on its way to collect Mum. Her stomach had bled in the night, she had tried to turn herself with the pain of vomiting blood and had fell out of bed onto the side where the sideboard still stood, she had ended up wedged between them, in a pool of her own blood. Alone in the dark.

Laura was unsure of how long she had been there, she was alerted by Rory barking, as he slept next to Mum downstairs.

I didn't realise it was physically possible to dress as quickly as I did that day.

Laura went with Mum in the ambulance, I arrived minutes later, Rugby St Cross, here I was again.

Mum was going to be alright, standing holding hands with Laura in the waiting room, I was finding it hard to comprehend how close I came to losing her that day, and that one day, maybe not that far in the future I would.

Mum had to remain in hospital for a number of weeks, Laura was still paid for this time and waited for Mum to be well enough to come home, I was so grateful for this, worried by who the next carer may be though.

I visited Mum every day, and with each visit she seemed to be brighter and more herself. A few weeks past and she was well enough to go home.

She had to come back by ambulance, both Laura and I were there to greet her and Tom came round straight from work.

Advised to reduce her alcohol consumption and change her over the counter painkillers to something paracetamol based only.

With Mum all settled back at home, and for the time being at least willing to follow the advice she had been given, it was a horrific scare, one powerful enough to keep Mum on the right track.

I felt less anxious and could focus my attention on my own life, what there was of it.

Unfortunately, my poor Nan's health was not in such a good way so my time and concerns went directly to her. She had what seemed like a bad cold, but was deathly pale and not strong enough to leave the house, which was most unlike my dear Nan, who although well into her eighties was very fit, sprightly in fact!

On my next visit, she was worse, nobody else had been in to see her, I could not get my Mum to her, to get a second opinion, so I took matters into my own hands and called out the doctor.

My Uncle who did visit her regularly was not impressed with my decision, even when they decided to take Nan into the small hospital in town and discovered that she was dangerously anaemic.

After a large blood transfusion she looked completely different, with colour back in her cheeks and lips.

It became evident that she had not been eating well at all. There were great concerns over her mental strength as well.

At this point my uncle did accept that Nan was not coping and thought maybe she should spend some of her time, during the week, when she was strong enough to return home, with him at his flat in Rugby.

Nan was not keen on this idea, protesting that she would be fine. Mostly she did not want to leave the village at all because she wouldn't be able to visit Mum whenever she wanted. I talked with her, it was so very sad for an independent old lady to have to admit to needing help, but she did. Albeit in a rather confused state.

It was so easy for me to visit Nan where she was though, being just round the corner from our house, I spent a great deal of time with her during this period. We talked and laughed, I always had spent a lot of time with her, sitting in her back yard or walking our dogs along the canal. She was a dear, simply soul my Nan, never had a luxury in her life. She did not complain or ever wish for what she didn't already have except for a healthy happy daughter.

Chapter 9

With Gary and I now in a better position money wise, as he now had a fulltime job, we talked about buying our own house. I had my reservations, given the cavernous holes in our relationship, but in true Rosie style, afraid to rock the boat, I went along with it. We established what our combined wages would allow us to borrow, what deposit we could pull together and armed with this information we commenced our search.

The small town we lived in was the obvious choice, knowing that on our limited budget, village properties were out of our reach.

We read details, compared everything and made a list of possibilities to view. We looked at so many I lost count. The process was not a quick one either. We were both working hard and I needed as much time as possible with my Mum.

My Nan was also back at home half of the time, spending a large amount of time with my uncle at his flat in Rugby, but when she was at home, I helped on a rota with my other uncle in keeping her well-fed.

Finally, after a number of weeks and much deliberation, Gary and I settled on a small mid terraced Victorian property, right in the centre of town. One in a row of four, looking over a school, and a church, with pathway and row of Beech trees directly in front, it was beautiful and quite a find within a town such as this.

We bought it as a three bed with a small downstairs bathroom, which we planned to rip out, making room for a utility and separate downstairs toilet. Then we planned to convert one of the upstairs rooms into a luxury bathroom.

As first time buyers we were in an excellent position, and the sale completed quickly and without a hitch.

We moved ourselves in a rented van. In order to help fund the move we sold our catering trailer and I too returned to working for others. In a not very pleasant factory and an even less pleasant place initially, but the money was good and I was never shy of hard work.

So we began a new chapter of our lives, I was optimistic, excited even about owning my own property again and the plans we had for our lovely old villa, work at the factory was a necessary evil that I could live with.

We started work on our plans almost immediately, a good friend was a very reputable plumber and he quickly had our beautiful Victorian bathroom fittings in place upstairs, so we could remove the old one.

I was very fond of the little house, I have always quickly grown to love certain places and had no feelings whatsoever for others!

Gary had set up a band with some local lads, they were pretty good too. They gigged in local pubs and clubs.

When I wasn't with them, I was happy at home alone with sometimes as many as five bottles of wine for company. I forced myself not to drink for two days of the week. These two days were complete torture, I think it was then that I fully realised how alcohol dependant I was. Quickly reasoning with myself that I had too much to cope with to not drink, and the two days of hell were not worth the stress!

That bottle was my best friend, my trusted companion. Drinking alone was my favourite thing to do.

The fun part about temping in a revolting factory is that they can end your employment, at any time, without warning. This is exactly what happened to me! Fuck I thought Gary is going to be less than impressed with this! We had a mortgage to pay, I needed work and fast.

A massive Argos Distribution Centre ran on one of the industrial estates in our town. From factory talk I had picked up that this Argos took on a great deal of temporary staff prior to Christmas each year, it was October. Without a second thought I drove directly to said Argos on release from the nasty factory. I was given an application form, I completed it there and then handed it in, received a phone call that evening and went for an induction the next day, then commenced employment the following Monday.

Conditions of work here, were far superior to the nasty factory, the pay was better, almost unlimited overtime and a small, very small chance of being made a permanent member of staff if you did well.

Well, I worked, I worked my little socks off! Never absent despite the enormity of some hangovers! My work was good and accurate, don't get me wrong, it was extremely menial, but the money and hours were brilliant.

I tried my absolute best to win that permanent position and I got it. That brown envelope was well deserved. Gosh I drank well that night!

Once permanent in my position at Argos I proceeded to learn as much as possible, trained in the different areas and to operate machinery. I soon gained respect from those above me and befriended many working with me. I was quite willing to work the different shift patterns.

My drinking continued at a spectacular level. My social life was on a high both with Gary or work colleagues.

Our little house was taking shape quite nicely. Gary and I went on some great camping trips and holidays, weekends away sometimes just the two of us and other times with friends.

On the whole and most definitely on the surface our lives were almost perfect.

For me though, beneath the outer show, there was still a little girl, who missed her Daddy every day, feared for the impeding loss of her mother and scared inside by men who did not love her the way she had been shown that love should be.

The inner sadness was on occasion almost impossible to

bear.

Mum bless her, had numerous carers come and go. Her one constant was her district nurse Becky, she a village lady, so Mum already knew her. Through all the carers that came and went Becky was there for her morning visit almost daily. Mum was so very fond of her as was I.

Mum's live in who came mostly after Laura was another lady called Rose, she was wonderful, and a more elderly lady who I just couldn't seem to completely trust, her care seemed good though and that was the main thing, as the monster Multiple Sclerosis was accelerating at an alarming rate.

Nan was seriously getting to the point where she needed to be in a care home, she wasn't of sound mind with consistency, so when on her own, she was a danger to herself and she was not content with my uncle on a permanent basis.

Her future care needed to be addressed at this point.

On one of my normal visits to Mum, nobody had phoned me which annoyed me somewhat and I expressed this. The Doctor had been called and all signs showed that Mum had had a small stroke. A lady already severely disabled by the chronic illness she had been fighting for decades, still only just 51 years old and completely reliant on others for every part of her wellbeing had now also had a stroke. This news didn't appear to upset Mum too much, but my golly did it upset me. This was all just so bloody unfair. My beautiful, strong, independent, funny Mum, supportive if me in every way was slipping away before my very eyes. I couldn't bear it.

Everything quite quickly went from bad to worse. Nan was put into the small local hospital once it was agreed that she was no longer able to care for herself, she remained there whilst a new permanent care home for the elderly could be found.

Every visit I made to Mum there seem to be a new problem to face, this time was so very difficult for us all. Tom who had his own family and work to deal with, was with her as much as possible. The same was true for me, I gave almost every spare minute I had to be with Mum, whilst working incredibly long hours at work to better my position there.

Gary was very supportive during this time, despite the fact that we spent very little time together.

A care home was found for my Nan in another village, quite central for all the people who would wish to visit her to be able to do so.

The main problem Nan had with this of course, was having no way to visit my Mum easily, although by this point, she was herself quite confused and would on occasion call me Jean. She was safe and well looked after though, it had a final feel to it. The times I had laughed and talked with my dear, always happy Nan were gone now and they would never return, I felt the loss long before she was gone.

Just before the Christmas of that year, Mum became very poorly, we put it down to flu, the doctor did come, but could only say the same. My Mum was not a well lady. Her speech by this time was almost incoherent, certainly so to those who did not know her well. She could not swallow properly. We gave her energy milkshakes through a straw.

As the days past her condition just worsened. We were powerless. On occasion she squeezed me back when I held her tight and struggled a smile for our benefit.

Mum always liked me to clean her teeth, said the carers never did a good job! I made sure I brushed her teeth, sponged her face and put perfume on for her before I left.

Leaving became extremely difficult, knowing that at any time it could be goodbye for the last time.

Meanwhile, my Nan's stay in the nursing home was a short one, she fell and hurt her hip so had to return to the small hospital in town. The nursing staff were wonderful there, I knew many of them well by this time, lovely ladies, finding the time often just to sit and talk to me. I was Nan's most regular visitor, they all remembered Mum well from her stay there. They were empathic to my life which was falling into pieces all around me.

Mum stayed with us through Christmas, but started to deteriorate rapidly after. I sat in Mum's kitchen on Boxing Day talking with Becky, I loved this lady "Rosie she has done this for you and Tom, stayed strong through Christmas, she did it for you, you do know that you mean the absolute world to her" I knew.

A few days later she was weaker than ever, the doctor was called, I made sure I was there.

The Doctor explained how Mum was a very tired lady, she was too weak to come back from this. We were told we had to let her go. We kept her at home, she was in the bed my father died in 17 years previous, we made her as comfortable as possible, all I could do was put her perfume on, they inserted a syringe driver, containing only water and morphine, she was given nothing else.

Nobody could tell us how long this would be for, maybe hours, maybe days, it was in fact the latter.

On day three, Gary took me over to see Mum, it was New Year's Eve, to my shock, Mum had her eyes slightly open, and she moved her hand when I held it and tried to speak. I sat for a very long time. These reactions from her I was not expecting to see again, this shook me rigid and on leaving the house I broke down "This isn't right, she is not ready to die, we are killing her!" I screamed and shook and screamed and shook some more and cried the tears of a lifetime of loss. Gary was very concerned, he knew I wasn't eating and my behaviour was out of control. He drove me to the Doctors and demanded we see someone.

We saw a Doctor I had known all of my life, he would call on occasion to visit my father, on a weekend, he came in tennis gear once, I never forgot that, when Doctors were real. He took my hand and explained very gently, the effects of morphine and how there is often a high before the final low. He calmed me down but he did not change my mind, I thought then and always have that we let my Mum go too soon.

Just waiting and holding her hand became the next few days. Every goodbye the last, every time the phone rang, my heart sank.

In the early hours of January the 4 th, at the age of 51 my dearest Mum lost her fight. The phone call did come, I had said my last goodbye, as we drove to the village I held my head and sobbed, it was a physical pain it hurt so much. A death not unexpected, but it carried with it, the enormity of unfairness, the suffering, the loss, Multiple Sclerosis is unforgiving and at 29 I had lost both my parents to its hands. I was inconsolable.

Tom and his wife, myself and Gary threw ourselves into arranging the funeral. We bought flowers for all the ladies who had been involved with Mum's care right to the end.

Tom and I took an emotional visit down to Becky's house, we were both very fond of her, and would be eternally grateful to that lovely lady. She was very upset herself, having cared for Mum for quite a number of years, she become an incredible friend to my Mum.

My first visit to Nan following Mum's death was one of the hardest things I have ever had to do. Family divided on whether or not she should even be told, as she was a confused old lady, I spoke with her key nurse, I was guided by her opinion that most definitely she should be told.

In a quiet room, alone with my Nan, staff waiting to help if need be, I held both her hands and looked her in the eye and told her that her daughter had died. She understood. She shook her head and sobbed saying only "my Jean, not my Jean, my dear Jean, it should have been me".

We held each other for a long time. On every visit after this one, my Nan called me Jean.

I stood on the landing of my childhood home as the hearse carrying my mother came solemnly down the road. The beautiful bouquet of white lilies, from Tom and I, covering the top. The service was in the village church which was full, Mum had lived in the village all her life and her family before her, many came to pay their respects.

Gary read a heartfelt tribute that we had written. I was a very broken lady that day.

As they laid her body to rest in the churchyard, into the grave that already held my father, only feet away from my granddad, I thought I would never smile again. All my smiles were in that hole in the ground.

Chapter 10

I took some time from work following the loss of my Mum, during which, I was with my Nan of a daytime and as thoroughly pissed as I could be of a night time.

On returning to work, I found it very difficult to concentrate on anything at all. My mind was a wash with loss, pain and the worry for my Nan who seemed to be slipping away from us fast. I visited her every single day. Every single day she seemed further away.

I was feeling so low that everyday life was drowning me. A very unhelpful Doctor decided in his wisdom to prescribe me prozac! Anybody with experience of this drug will know that, if it is going to be of any help at all that it takes you lower first. I also do not believe that anti-depressant drugs should be used for bereavement.

My alcohol consumption was just stupidly high, eating very little and taking this new drug.

Gary and I were on the edge of disaster the whole time, his temper coupled with my 'depression' which was of course bereavement and gallons of booze, made our alone time explosive.

One evening when Gary returned from the pub to find me huddled on a chair listening to music and crying into my bottle of beer, he erupted, every bit of me that he could throw back at me was. My drinking being central to all of his verbal attack. He broke bottles on the floor and left me huddled on the same chair surrounded by broken glass with nothing on my feet and very very drunk!

I negotiated the glass, found my bag and left the house, heading straight for the taxi rank.

My taxi took me to the village, to Mum's house sitting empty, of course I asked the driver to go via the off licence.

I sat in the sitting room, glass in one hand, cigarette in the other and contemplated life or death.

I had one very important person left, my Nan, for her the answer was life.

I remained at Mum's empty house for three weeks, my only visitors were Mum's neighbour whom I had known all of my life and Somer, a brilliant friend from Argos, she was amazing at this time, I don't know if I could have got through without her.

Then one night I was again very low and Gary phoned offering the love and protection I so badly needed. He collected me and all my things, I never slept another night in that house.

Two weeks later my dear old Nan passed away. Peacefully, in the care of the wonderful ladies at the cottage hospital in town.

Funeral arrangements were all taken care of by my uncles (who had no love for each other) so I was relieved not to be part of that process.

On the day of the funeral, all close relatives gathered in Nan's kitchen waiting for the hearse to come. As Gary and I entered, my Sister in law looked from me to Tom, with an expression that simply said "they shouldn't be going through this again".

The service was once again beautiful and to a packed church. I wore the same clothes as to Mum's, my tears were very fresh though and my heart now completely broken.

As her body was taken down to rest with my grand dad, in the village graveyard, we had to walk past the grave of my mother and father, at this point I just dissolved, Gary practically had to hold me up. My mind, my body and my soul could take no more. I wished I could disappear, from that place, from the pain that burned deep inside of me like an uncontrollable fire.

The weeks that followed were torture, from that second when you wake, when you open your eyes and it's another day, then the tidal wave hits you carrying the reminder of loss, the finality of it all, I found it almost impossible just to make it through the day.

Gary booked us a holiday in Scotland, he thought it would do me good to get away. Scotland, my favourite place on earth, I didn't argue. On a chilly day with an empty heart, I walked with him up Glen Nevis and there he asked me to marry him. I did not have the strength to give the right answer, so I said yes. Inverness was where we ended our trip, at a tiny jewellers there on the river, I bought myself a beautiful gold bracelet with the money that was left in Mum's bank account, I was also bought an engagement ring for a wedding I knew should never happen.

Thomas and I sold Mum's house, I wanted to keep it and just give Tom his half from the sale of our little town house, Gary wouldn't hear of it. I was devastated, my childhood home being sold when it could easily have been ours; it felt like the final nail in an already massive coffin.

As hard as I tried I could no longer see a purpose for my life. I had agreed to marry another man who would take his hand to me, and reduced my confidence to pulp on a daily basis. I felt my existence was meaningless and too painful to continue with.

On a bank holiday weekend, when Gary's brother was staying with us, we went on a night out in town, we all drank excessively, I thought it would be better to take myself away to my parents on a night when Gary would not wake up to just me in the house. When the others had gone to bed, I took my stash of paracetamol from the cupboard and my hidden bottle of favourite wine. Alone in that dark room, with silent tears stinging my cheeks I took the lot.

The next thing I remember was Gary's voice yelling at me but it sounded muffled. I heard his brother shout over him "stop Gaz just get her in the car!"

Next thing I remember, was lying in a hospital bed, Gary sat next to me with his head in his hands.

When he realised I was awake he grabbed my hand "I thought I'd lost you" there was genuine hurt in his eyes, I felt guilty for causing this pain. I had to stay in hospital for the rest of the weekend, mostly Gary was with me. I also had a lovely lady come and talk with me. She made me see things from a different view, that the grieving would not last forever and it would be replaced by happy memories. That the last thing my parents would want was for me to be unhappy and that the very last thing they would want was for me to take my own life.

Through the summer of that year, exciting things happened. We had an offer for our house, as did our three neighbours, from a large food retailer. We were to receive a substantial sum, well above the market value with all expenses paid. Now as much as I loved our little house, this gave opportunity for a return to the village and as I also had my share of Mum's house to add to the pot, we would be looking at some rather lovely properties.

Before the house move, however we had of course the wedding to plan. We were fortunate enough to between us be able to spend a fair amount of money. Location we chose, was a nearby golf course Hotel, where we could marry, have the reception and a honeymoon suite for that night. Very nice it was too!

Kate and Somer were to be my bridesmaids, with Tom under duress, to give me away, again.

I chose a beautiful silk, fitted, baby pink dress, with gorgeous flowers to complement my outfit. We decided upon a hot lunch for our day guests, with an evening buffet too. The whole day was going to be so flash that I got swept along by it all, pushing firmly to the back of my head the feeling that I knew damn well I should not be marrying the man at all!

Scotland for two weeks, staying in different hotels was to be our honeymoon. This I was looking forward to, and dreading in equal measures. Scotland is so beautiful, photographers dream. Drinking all the time though would cause us to disagree. I would have absolutely no escape and would somehow need to maintain 'honeymooning duties' the part of our relationship that I was finding increasingly difficult.

In the beginning our sex life was pretty good, not screaming from the roof tops curling your toes good, but pretty good. The more a person hurts you, physically and, or emotionally, the less you want to share your body with that person. So for me, orgasms had become very much a solo sport!

Wedding day number two arrived, I woke up with a desperate desire to run away, I didn't.

Kate, Somer and myself looked gorgeous. The men looked like men. The necessary words were said. The expected photographs were taken. Touching and amusing speeches were made. Expensive food was eaten. I was under strict orders not to drink too much, I paced myself quite nicely and by the end of the evening I was proud to be the most sober person in the room.

Gary was pissed out of his head and I was saved from

wedding night sexual expectations.

The following morning however there was tension between us already, thankfully we had arranged to breakfast with the few guests that stayed over.

Immediately after a mediocre hotel breakfast we set off up north. I love car journeys, loud music and wonderful views on this one from the top of the M6 onwards.

Good time to reflect also, I had nobody else to blame this time, I was not a naive twenty year old, I had lived with this man for a number of years. Why oh why Rosie do you never have the strength when you need it most? I scolded myself for my pathetic weakness, for fearing what the word no would have meant. A simple honest answer to his proposal would, yes have been difficult at first, in the fullness of time though, peace would have been mine, but no, I married, I must lie in the bed I made for myself.

Our honeymoon was pretty much how I expected it would be. A mix of wonderfulness, tension, beauty, annoyance, love and hate.

Two weeks that passed very quickly with a great amount of photographs that put together, painted a lovely picture.

Once home we had the task of finding a new home, as the development planned for ours was moving quite quickly. Our possibilities ranged from a brand new typical characterless four bed detached in town, to cottages with views and personalities in the surrounding villages.

Nothing really pulled at my heart though.

Then one day on a drive through the village after visiting the graves, I saw a for sale sign, on the cottage right next to the one my Nan and Granddad owned, where my Mum had been born in fact.

Driving directly to the estate agents I booked a viewing without even reading the details.

I showed Gary the info and was as keen as I, after all the cottage was on the village green directly opposite a pub, a good pub, a pub his band played in regularly.

I viewed the property on my own the next morning before my shift at work. It was empty, having been renovated for sale, it was perfect in every way, a new house with some old features still in place. I knew without doubt this was where I wanted to live.

Gary viewed it later the same day and we were both agreed, the white house on the village green was for us.

The sale went without hitch and before Christmas of that same year we moved ourselves. It was a long day, we had no help, so lifting and carrying left me exhausted and hungry. I wanted to sit on a box, with pizza and a glass of wine and laugh at each other, like they do in the movies. Gary went to the pub. I sat on the kitchen counter with my wine, no pizza, no laughing, it was the nicest kitchen I had ever had though.

We moved on a Friday, by the end of that weekend our house looked perfect, everything in place, Daddy's paintings on the walls, Denby in the kitchen and matching bedding in all the right rooms. I did really love it, and to be back in the village was such a joy, to be able to walk my little dog Marshall out the front door and be by the cut in minutes, escaping opportunities galore!

Having spare rooms for people to stay, opened up our social calendar somewhat and knowing people from school who drank in the pub opposite brought us a whole new set of friends.

The best of these was a couple, both from the village, the girl the same age as me, Daisy and the guy a few years older, Matthew. They were engaged to be married. Gary got on well with them too, so they soon became firm friends and many an enjoyable evening was spent either, with them at their home, them at ours or us all in the pub for a meal and a night out.

Gary's band was doing well, they played often, which gave him immense pleasure and me too, live music in a pub was my most favoured night out.

All these aspects of our life in the village made our relationship better at first. I still had doubt in my heart though where Gary was concerned and worse than that, fear too.

Work was going really well for me, I had progressed to one of the staff trainers, I loved this role and shared it with another girl a year older than I, who married a village guy. Steph was great, we had such a laugh at work, we covered for each other when necessary, she lived in town, so we never socialised together at all, but both shared a love of booze, so were well equipped to deal with each other's hangovers, even to the point of a short nap in the office when needed!

I did also spend many a solitary hour with only a bottle of wine for company. Thinking about my mother, my dear Nan and of course my very special Daddy. My Daddy that never knew me as an adult, missed all my important Birthdays, never gave me away at either of my weddings or given me the strength to make the right choices, as I was sure he would have done.

Walking, oh my did I do a lot of walking, around the paths I had walked with my Nan. Down the fields that gave my father inspiration for some of his paintings. Occupants of some locally moored narrow boats became familiar faces for a chat. I walked for miles sometimes, always Marshall and me, I talked to that little rescue dog like a best friend, thinking thank goodness he can never tell my secrets.

Gary remained, unpredictable after alcohol, angered easily if I drank to excess and always moody. It was like waiting to decide what mood I was going to be allowed to be in, governed always by him. I feared my husband so even when smiling and having fun I was never really happy. On the surface we had it all, but scratch a little deeper and the truth was very different.

Chapter 11

Now it is safe to say we had some mighty fine times living in our house on the Green. Our good friends Matt and Daisy's wedding was a wonderful day.

Seeing in the new millennium on our balcony surrounded by friends was amazing.

Our big summer barbecue on our extensive patio with many family and friends was talked about for weeks after.

I was given the accolade of best breakfast ever by a beautiful friend who sadly lost his life to Cancer only months after.

But … there also was many a time I was locked out in the middle of the night, saved by my lovely neighbours sofa.

I ran away on many a night, saved by my lovely neighbours sofa.

Police were called on a night when I feared for my life and I was locked in.

All of these occasions were completely and utterly my fault, as I was too drunk to handle and I invited him to hit, push and verbally destroy me! I was told this for quite some time. Years in fact.

My grieving became something I had I was to do alone. One Sunday morning I was particularly upset about Mum, Dad and my Nan, it was all overflowing on that morning, I sat on the sofa in our gorgeous sitting room, crying. Gary was lying on the floor with the Sunday paper, after some time he turned to me "for fuck sake Rosie stop snivelling, I'm trying to read!" I took the dog out.

Two years I lived in that wonderful house, living the dream and the nightmare all at the same time.

One day, I got the flu, nasty it was, not a bad cold, proper flu. I was in bed for a couple of days, I could not even drink a drop of booze, that's how bad it was!

On one of these nights Gary went on a mad one, in town with some work mates, he got home at stupid o'clock thoroughly wankered, I was in bed but not sleeping, my heart began to race as he came up the stairs, he was always such a bastard when he was pissed.

This night was no exception, except this night I had not had a drink, I was not well at all.

Gary finally got into bed after negotiating the bathroom and his clothes, he got in beside me, pulled at the duvet and then kicked me right in the middle of my back so hard it winded me and I landed on the floor.

I got up off the floor, took my tissues and my orange

juice and went into the spare room, I never got into that bed again.

We had talked of splitting up before, but had always resolved to stay together. This time was different. The morning after that kick, I knew for sure that I was not to blame for his violence, I was not to blame for his anger and I was not going to change my mind.

I told him we were over, finished, no more and I meant every word. The house was on the market within a week and I started divorce proceedings on the grounds of unreasonable behaviour.

The worst of this was that he had nowhere else to live and neither did I, so for the entire time it took to sell the house we both lived in it. In our separate bedrooms, leading our separate lives.

It took a year to sell that house!

It was crazy really, as was our whole relationship, during that year I cooked for him sometimes, we even holidayed together; he also had me up against the wall with his hands round my throat! I think he even scared himself that time.

Eventually our house sold, I found a tiny cottage that I could afford on my own in my village. The people buying our house on the green were selling a modern house on the new estate in the village, the couple selling the tiny cottage I was to buy bought the modern house that our purchasers were selling, we were in a circle, not a chain so after such a long wait the sale actually went smoothly.

Working in a warehouse full of men, definitely had its draw backs but its bonuses too.

In my role as staff trainer, as long as I wore safety shoes, what I wore was up to me, so on mainly office bound days, with my safety court shoes on I could dress rather well.

Lots of men trapped in an environment for quite a number of hours meant that they admired the females around them more than they would say in the pub on a Friday night! This all concluded to me having a number of, especially younger blokes having the eye for me.

One young lad in particular made no secret of this fact. Sean, nothing to look at and over ten years younger than me, was a gentle lad, very hard working and pleasant enough, I was not attracted to him though in any way.

On one of our many work nights out, just before Christmas of that year, having drunk my usual gallon of alcohol, on leaving the pub we were all in, I stumbled slightly in the doorway and Sean caught my arm.

This night out was the start of my relationship with Sean Robinson.

On moving day to my little cottage near the canal, Sean was there to help me.

That day was horrible, I was leaving a beautiful extensive home, with lovely views and right next door to my Mum's family home for a tiny cottage in need of work. I left myself money to complete the work I wanted doing but it was such a massive step down, a step back, as I cleaned my en suite shower in that gorgeous house I cried.

Only a house however, I knew I could make the little cottage lovely so I bounced back quickly and carried on.

Within a matter of months my little cottage was taking shape quite nicely and felt like home.

Sean and I were together and very happy, although not madly in love with him, this man was the complete opposite of everything I had had in a partner before. Nothing I did was wrong in his eyes, I was allowed to make decisions about what we did. He never raised his voice, he never argued, he understood why my drinking was the way it was and just looked after me when necessary, without criticism.

I felt happy and contented for the first time in a long time.

With Sean and I both working at Argos on the same shift, life was stress free, we were financially stable, content both at home and at work. The cottage was of course mine though and I was more than capable and happy to manage the mortgage and household bills myself. All Sean had to do was give me a percentage of his wages to cover our food.

As time passed with Sean, there were no surprises, good ones or otherwise, I welcomed the calm stability of our relationship. Even after a year together Sean was as doting as he had ever been, the only thing that suffered for this was my nice trim size 12 figure!

Being in my early thirties and having always wanted children, but never having had a man who deserved to be a father, I thought more and more about starting a family. Sean too was eager to have children despite only being young himself.

There seemed no reason to wait, we were both happy and settled so I started to make plans and very importantly for the first time in my adult life found a good reason to cut down on alcohol.

I decided, being a person who likes to plan, that a child born at the start of the school year would have advantage over those born in the summer, so, steps to conceive needed to be taken after Christmas. Folic acid and healthy food already on the menu.

Almost to order, I was extremely lucky to be expecting my first child at the end of the November of that year.

Overjoyed an understatement, after all that life had thrown my way, this baby really was going to be a gift, the most precious and loved baby, I hated pregnancy, I worried excessively, just counting the days to hopefully meet my healthy little baby.

I remained at work for as long as possible, to give us a good start financially, as I had no intention of returning to work, knowing that changes at Argos would make it possible for me to take voluntary redundancy on the closure of my maternity leave.

After the onset of pre-eclampsia late in my pregnancy, I was taken into be induced two weeks prior to my due date.

Almost 36 hours later, out came my beautiful baby girl. Everything I had ever wanted I had in my arms. There were complications with my birth which required us to remain in hospital for 4 days.

This was such an overwhelming time, nothing can prepare you for the instant love you have for your own child. My perfect little baby girl, we named her Amy Jean, Jean after the grandmother she would never get to meet, the pain of that was almost unbearable too, my mother's unquestionable love for me, would have extended immediately to my own daughter, the loss of that love was a void in our lives.

Sean was every bit the adoring father, he took two weeks from work and during this time he took on the household chores happily and every part of our baby's care that he could. I was breastfeeding Amy though and from the moment she arrived home she did not seem to sleep for more than a couple of hours at a time.

My health visitor and midwives were wonderful support but despite all our best efforts my baby just did not settle into a routine. It was thought she had colic, we dealt with this accordingly. Then it was suggested that she had intolerance to lactose so we put her onto a bottle feed of Soya milk. Amy still did not settle easily and woke many times throughout the night. Her cot was next to our bed, but out of sheer exhaustion I let her sleep next to me as it was the only place she seemed content.

I loved my baby with my whole heart but for reasons nobody could not explain I suffered with post natal depression. My health visitor was simply amazing; I don't know how I would have managed without her. Having no family to help really was very difficult, Sean's mother was a very selfish individual who gave us no help whatsoever, I missed my own Mum immensely at this point, strongly believing that things would have been very different indeed, had she still been with us.

From my experience post natal depression is a very lonely place, a place where you feel guilt and self-loathing. With the right support I was able to overcome this, but it was a lengthy and painful process. It's a baffling unkind condition, not to be left without help.

Nothing however could take away the all-consuming, unconditional love and adoration that I had for my daughter Amy Jean.

Chapter 12

As my daughter grew, so did I. Wanting nothing but the best for her, I started to think ahead, deciding that when she became school age I would like to have the same surname as her. My desire for her to have a sibling was also important to me. Considering all these factors I concluded that Sean and I should marry and then try for a second child.

In the September of Amy's first year, Sean and I married at a hotel in Scotland, I planned the whole thing, paid for Sean's mother and partner to come as witnesses and with little Amy there too, the day was very special. I never felt a deep burning love for Sean but he worked hard, he was kind. A good father, too, mostly anyway, with my guidance, he, wasn't well, very dynamic shall we say. All decision making and responsibility was left entirely to me, but he was not capable of hurting me and never made me feel anything less than special, a feeling I hadn't known before.

During this time of relative contentment I gained a lot of weight, drank probably too heavily, but in comparison to earlier years, it was moderate. Amy continued to be hard work, mine was always the child who didn't listen at parties, always the one who seemed to have tantrums bigger than the other children. I did think I must be a terrible parent!

With the exception of Amy being hard to handle and only sleeping in our bed, our life was wonderful. I loved my little cottage and its location, although there was the thought in my head that a larger home would be needed in a few years if we were to be blessed with another child. Sean now worked in a different place on a rotating shift system that sometimes left me exhausted dealing with Amy on my own at night whilst Sean worked, likewise trying to keep her quite whilst he slept during the day. The pay was worth the inconvenience and meant that being careful with money I could stay at home with Amy, something I was keen to do at all costs, as having no grandparents to help, I was not leaving her so young in a nursery unless absolutely necessary, which thankfully it wasn't.

That Christmas, with Amy just over a year old, with some sort of routine, was lovely, we were quite an insular little family with the exception of visits to Tom's for special occasion meals, we spent our time at home, just the three of us.

I stood in the garden one evening, glass in hand and raised it high, speaking to my parents, of how I wished they were with us, how proud I knew they would be of Amy and of my loneliness without them. They were never far from my thoughts, when Amy was a challenge I would beg my Mum for guidance.

Friendships were important to me and two wonderful ones had been rekindled after the isolation I had been put into by Andrew, and never in the same social circle of that I had with Gary, Kate also had a boy slightly older than Amy and herself hoped to have more children and also India, she too had a boy of similar age, so we started to meet at parks with the children, it was a joyous time, picnics in parks with beautiful friends, watching your children play. Such a far cry from my earlier years of drunken debauchery!

For a number of months our lives continued along this ilk, there was no concern of moving at this point and I wanted more of an age gap to be thinking of a second child. We managed for money, far from well off, but we lived a simple life and this we could afford. I still questioned my parenting skills, as Amy seemed more wilful almost daily and pushed me to my limit. My beliefs on raising a child were such that I would never resort to even a slight smack, I tried hard not to shout and followed guidelines from my health visitor, but still I felt I was failing.

Despite my struggle with Amy's behaviour, I totally loved motherhood, I baked, we made shapes in the sandpit, had tea parties with teddies and cuddly dogs, walked for miles laughing at the names of canal boats and playing poo sticks under the bridges, collecting leaves to make pictures, reading books for hours, every part I loved, feeling only that I wished I could do a better job and to share these joys with my lost family.

The Christmas after Amy's second birthday we started to try for another baby. As with Amy this proved an easy task and very soon all was well and in place for daughter number two to be born at the end of that year. We were both thrilled, my only concern was how on earth was I going to cope with a new-born and my very headstrong toddler!

Pregnancy was most uncomfortable, in my new bloomed over weight state, I struggled the whole way through, basically eating way too much and resting way too much! Amy had by now started at the village pre school, this did mean I had a few hours each day to myself and I felt it immensely beneficial to her, being around other children and learning at the same time.

Nearing the end of my pregnancy, as I was clinically obese by now, the powers to be decided that my baby was very large and it seemed unlikely that I would be able to have a natural birth if she grew any larger, so two weeks prior to my due date I was taken in to be induced. This proved to be a terrible decision and after a horrific time Isabelle Rose was born, she was not large at all, she was completely perfect.

Once again, due to the emergency section I had and enormous blood loss, I remained in the high dependency unit for a few days, then a few more days on a ward before I could go home. Sean had taken leave from work so the first two weeks were relatively easy, although it was apparent immediately that I had another daughter who would avoid sleep at all costs and cry uncontrollably for what seemed like no reason.

Majority of Isabelle's quiet time was spent on one of my breasts! Amy did not like her little sister one bit at this stage as her Mummy had been taken over!

These issues settled with time, except for Belle not sleeping, for more than two hours at a time day or night. It was exhausting and wonderful at the same time.

Sean and I were completely alone in the upbringing of our girls, his Mother had removed herself from our lives following an argument between herself and Sean, which I tried to rectify, but after being let down on so many occasions it was agreed between my health visitor and myself that she was causing more harm than good and should be given no more opportunities. Sad though it was, for my two gorgeous daughters to have no grandparents at all,but it was the reality of our situation.

In early spring of Isabelle's first year and Amy was three years old, we went on holiday, to Cornwall in a beautiful detached bungalow, with its own large private garden. It was lovely, very picturesque and luxury compared with our little cottage. On the first night there, I became quite ill, with sickness and intense pain, that felt like indigestion but far more powerful. Throughout the holiday I suffered and was really perplexed as to what the cause of such horrific pain could be.

On our return home I saw my Doctor and was referred for tests which quickly confirmed that I had gallstones. I was advised to eat a very low fat diet and awaited the date for minor surgery to have them removed.

I started to notice; with the health issue that I had to deal with that Sean was very reluctant to even make a simple phone call to Doctors or anything regarding the house whatsoever. All responsibility fell on my shoulders and having two very young children the weight of this started to take its toll on our relationship. Especially as we had decided that we needed a larger home, only having two bedrooms, one of which that was very small and a downstairs bathroom, my little cottage that I so adored, we had outgrown, so I proceeded to make enquiries with estate agents and the bank to see what our options where. Entirely in my hands this task was. My hands were already pretty full!

Still having to be strict with my diet and also feeling extremely unwell at times, I sorted out the finances available to us for a move and started searching for a suitable property.

Priority was to stay in the village if at all possible which meant most likely we would be looking at an ex local authority dwelling. This did not concern me, location of greatest importance, so the girls could attend the village school, and size.

We found the perfect house, three bed roomed semi-detached, with a huge garden, in a quiet spot on the very edge of the village. Finding a buyer for our little cottage took some time, but eventually all was in place. At the end of that summer we moved into the home I hoped we could remain in for the rest of our lives.

Both girls found the move extremely difficult, new surroundings and a change in so many ways was overwhelming for them, with much reassurance and lots of extra cuddles they began to settle. Isabelle still not sleeping well and Amy's behaviour becoming increasingly difficult, I was worried for my impending surgery for gallstones, knowing that leaving them even with their own father for more than a few hours was a challenge for them all.

When the day of my surgery arrived, it was planned as a day case and really went incredibly smoothly and I was back with my family by the evening, which as Belle was still feeding from me at night, was a great relief.

I recovered quickly, leaving only four tiny scares.

This health scare however turned my head into the right direction health wise, I continued with the low fat diet I had become used to and hoped to lose a mighty five stone in weight. I set my mind to this goal and also making our new house a home. Spending as much time as possible with my daughters.

Life was good, I hoped my bubble would never burst. I was mistaken.

Chapter 13

Almost immediately, on return to pre-school, after the summer break, a wonderful member of their staff asked to talk with me. Amy had exhibited some worrying behaviours, so much so that they were to refer her to the Educational Psychologist. Completely dumbfounded, I asked what she believed might be the problem, on a purely personal level, as she had a family member with the same, she mentioned, Asperger Syndrome, part of the Autistic Spectrum.

This news destroyed me. I cried, almost constantly for a week. Then my research began, I needed to know everything I could about this condition I knew nothing of. I bought books and read them cover to cover. Searched the internet, making notes. It became my only focus, to find out as much information as I possibly could, if this was my daughter's condition I needed to help her, make her life as easy as it could be.

Amy was scheduled for a two day assessment at the child development centre at the general hospital. I made notes and wrote down everything that I thought could possibly be of use to them about my daughter and her ways.

Whilst reading about Asperger Syndrome in one of the better books, it was like light bulbs being switched on in my head. All the behaviour problems, the differences between Amy and the other children, slotted into place.

Everything made sense. My little girl was Autistic.

Now at this time Belle was just a year old. On one of my cleaning job days, a Thursday it was, Amy was at pre-school and Isabelle stayed at home with her father. When I returned home I could see instantly that something was not right with Isabelle, she could put no weight on her arm when crawling, Sean said she had a little fall on the bottom of the stairs but he thought she was fine. Something in her face also alarmed me, she had lost all colour and seemed very distressed. I phoned the National Health Service helpline which was in operation then. They advised me to take her to the local accident and emergency department.

When we all got there, they arranged for Isabelle to have an x ray. After this we were put in a side room to wait for the Doctor to come and see us.

After a lengthy wait, I complained, we had two young daughters, one of them in pain with a possible break and we were just left waiting, it made no sense.

After a great deal of confusion, different people asking us questions, most of whom we could hardly understand what they were even saying. Belle's arm was put into a tiny pink cast and I was asked to take her back to the hospital the following morning to attend fracture clinic.

The fracture clinic was very well run, unlike the emergency department! I saw a lovely English Doctor, he thoroughly examined Isabelle and looked at her x ray, he agreed it was broken and a more permanent cast was put in place. He shook my hand as I left and said to me

"I can see what's happened here, we should be able to draw a line under this quite quickly".

Now, I know I should have questioned what he meant be this, but at the time I was keen to get Isabelle back for her lunch and to collect Amy. So I just left.

That Friday afternoon, around four o'clock I received a phone call. Social Services! They asked if Sean, myself and the girls could be at home as they planned to visit within the hour. I called Sean back from work, although shocked by the serious nature of the call, nothing could have prepared me for what was about to happen.

Before five o'clock on that Friday afternoon, a lady from Social Services and a lady police officer knocked on our door.

They told me that the x ray of Isabelle's arm showed a previous break, an unreported break.

I gasped trying to take in what they were saying, I broke as I said the words "you think I might have hurt my daughter?"

It was explained that we were to be placed on a family order, which meant, that, we were not to be left alone with the children, so unless we could find friends or relatives to stay with us for the weekend, the children would be taken into care.

I dissolved, ran to bathroom and was violently ill.

They explained that the x ray had to be checked by

Birmingham Children's Hospital, as requested by the Doctor I saw that morning at fracture clinic.

I told them that it was absolutely not possible for there to be a previous break, I would have known. As a parent who had never once smacked even, I simply could not digest what they were suggesting may be the case. With the threat of losing our children, I could not function, I held Belle to my chest and cried.

The phone rang, it was my Health visitor, she told me both her and our Doctor had written reports stating that at no point had there ever been an issue with our children's health or safety, the opposite in fact.

Her words to me are etched on my heart "my darling you are on a train and you cannot get off until it reaches its destination, the first Doctor you saw at the Emergency department who looked at the x ray, believed there was an earlier break and set a ball in motion that cannot be stopped until all procedures are followed, but it will stop, you just have to be strong until it does".

I called Tom, he and his wife came straight over. My health visitor too came on her way home, she hugged me and we both cried, she explained that she had done all she could do, she was as wonderful as ever and without her support I fear I would have crumbled even more.

Tom thought I was taking it all too seriously, of course knowing me, he even told the Social worker how ridiculous it all was as I completely spoilt my girls and Tom put all their behaviour issues down to me being too soft on them! They left as soon as I could get Kate over for the night. They had told me that we could be visited at any time to check that we were not alone with the girls, and action would be taken if they found us to be. Despite Tom's dismissal of the situation, I could not take any risks and as my Health visitor said, I simply must do what they asked of us.

Kate was fantastic, she slept on the sofa downstairs, I could not let Isabelle out of my sight, I was quite literally worried sick for the entire weekend. Kate could not stay the whole day having family of her own to care for, so a dear friend at the time came all the way from Salisbury on the Saturday to spend that night with us.

It was nothing but pure hell that weekend, whilst I was confident that nothing had ever happened to Belle's arm to cause her the discomfort she had exhibited with this break, it spun round and round in my head, what if she had broken it and I hadn't known, it could have been possible, she was not a settled baby, bless her, what if thrashing around in her cot had caused a damage I was unaware of.

The worry was intense, I couldn't eat or sleep and never seem to dry of tears.

Without a question this weekend was the worst of my entire life.

We had booked four nights away to a caravan in Devon for my birthday, due to leave that Monday and had been told we were not allowed to go until the x ray had been checked by the specialist at Birmingham Children's Hospital, I was given the name of a lady doctor at Rugby whom I could communicate with to check progress as they were aware of this situation causing much stress. Stress? Fuck me they had absolutely no idea!

I phoned the lady at Rugby every two hours, each time she was helpful and sympathetic, she actually arranged for a taxi to take my daughter's x ray direct to the hospital in Birmingham.

On the Sunday my friend from Salisbury had to drive back with her two boys who had camped out on my sitting room floor! The boys had thought this was an amazing adventure and despite all the turmoil, we managed to keep the weekend fun for the children.

My dear friend India came on the Sunday to stay with me, still phoning for news every two hours; it seemed the x ray was just sitting waiting for someone in high enough authority to look at it! Whilst I internally tore myself to shreds with what felt like a death sentence hanging over my head!

Middle of that sunny October Sunday the lady from Rugby hospital telephoned me, as the nice Doctor at fracture clinic had suspected, what the original A&E man had thought was an old break was simply the shadow of the current one, the family order was lifted, and with an inadequate verbal apology, our nightmare was over, I sobbed and sobbed.

Nothing comes close to love you have for your own children. That weekend is like another scar and the enormity of its pain never forgotten.

Monday morning we packed up the car, off to Devon, trying to maintain the schedule of events that I now knew Amy needed, because although not yet formally diagnosed, I felt for certain that she was autistic. All the pieces fitted together.

The pain in my heart from the weekend still remained and I not for one second let Isabelle out of my sight. I slept with Isabelle, spending many hours in the dark just watching her, feeling her breath against my face.

On our return home my over protection of my little girl continued, I slept on an airbed in her room, next to the mattress I had on the floor for her because I didn't want to even take the risk of her falling out of bed.

My concern for Amy also remained prominent; I had a little girl whose whole world was confusing for her. The date was set for early the next year when she would go for a two day assessment at hospital, to be seen from specialists, and then a diagnosis would be given.

I felt in control of Amy's condition though, many helpful books and websites had given me the knowledge to do my very best for her and make everyday life a joy and not a trial.

The weekend of my nightmare with Belle had left me basically distraught in so many ways, it rocked my confidence as a parent, I was unable to think any further than my girls. Sean was proving to be pretty damn useless, yes he worked hard but that was it, responsibility for all other things was down to me, I felt lonely, and troubled.

One night as I lay on the floor in the dark next to Belle, I noticed a flashing in the corner of my vision in my left eye. Since the weekend with Belle I also had tinnitus in both ears. Some tremors in my hands, also pins and needles in my hands and feet.

Silent tears crept down my cheeks, all these symptoms were oh so familiar to me, I wanted to scream, how much more can one person take I thought, feeling sick to the pit of my stomach I knew I had all the early signs of Multiple Sclerosis.

I kept my fears and feelings about the possible MS to myself for a while, concentrating on the children and day to day issues, anything to take it out of my head, but it wouldn't go, I made an appointment to see my Doctor. I didn't tell anybody.

On Amy's forth Birthday I made a pact with myself to shed that extra five stone in weight, I had already lost a couple of stone but I was determined more than ever to be more health conscience.

On the day of my Doctor's appointment I felt a deep hurt, I already felt I knew the answers, I was very stretched, dealing with so much at this time, Sean was of no use whatsoever, he distanced himself from everything, being either at work or fishing!

My Doctor, when I told her of my symptoms, although thinking it most unlikely to be MS, given my family history referred me directly to a Neurologist.

I drove from the Doctors to the grave of my parents, I sat

on the grass and stared at their headstone, my thoughts we fractured and so was my heart, how could this be happening, how was I going to cope, I was so lost and so alone, my life was crumbling around me.

I bought extra wine on my way home, hoping the answers would come from the bottom of the second one.

Chapter 14

I went to my Neurologist appointment on my own, he was a distant character, he had no time for my emotions, he did a basic examination and then, he did given my family history, order the three diagnostic tests to be done as soon as was possible, these three tests are a MRI scan, a lumber puncture and an Evoked Potentials test.

I left his office and walked down the crowded corridor back towards the car feeling lonely and terrified.

Music volume high in the car I drove home in tears.

Flashing through my mind, memories of the pain, disability and degrading shit that my dear parents had been through was now heading my way. I had to deal with it, and deal with it well, my girls were more important to me than anything and as their father was proving to be increasingly useless, it was down to me.

I pushed my impending tests to the back of my mind, as the dates had come through for Amy's two day hospital assessment. I started a diary of her behaviour, to take with me to the appointment. We also had a home visit from one of the assessment assistant's, she was lovely, Amy warmed to her immediately, as she did with everybody, she had on one occasion just hugged a random man in Sainsburys just because he smiled! Amy's emotions were often exaggerated and inappropriate. The visit helped us both to be better prepared for what was to come at the hospital.

On the first day of Amy's assessment, we arrived early, always my preference, I hate to be late or rushed.

The day was a day of Amy being observed in normal play and broken up by professionals making their observations.

Amy enjoyed the first day and the second. She returned to normal pre-school for the remainder of the week. I anxiously awaited the results which we had to return for in two weeks' time.

My diet was going wonderfully. Still reading as much as possible about Amy's condition. I still slept next to Isabelle's bed on the floor. Trying not to think about MS at all. Sean continued to be a useless twat.

The day arrived for us to return to the hospital to receive their assessment and maybe a diagnosis for Amy.

I was unsure really what to expect, I knew Amy had profound differences to other children, but on the two days we had been there I thought she was extremely well behaved and felt they hadn't really seen my true Amy.

However, we were read the report, my health visitor was with me, and then at the end the top man looked at me directly "I can confirm that with all the evidence we have seen in addition to your report and that of Amy's pre-school, that Amy has Asperger Syndrome which is part of the Autistic Spectrum. Now no matter how you prepare for something such as this, when a professional sits in front of you and tells you, it is like being hit by a fucking great big truck!

Loaded with various pieces of literature to help us and a copy of the report I left that hospital as the mother of an autistic child. There is quite a process that comes with any diagnosis of this kind, a kind of grieving period for the child you thought you had and to accept the child that you do have.

Somebody gave me this and it helped me enormously -

Welcome to Holland

I am often asked to describe the experience of raising a child with a disability – to try to help people who have not shared that unique experience to understand it, to imagine how it would feel. It's like this…

When you're going to have a baby, it's like planning a fabulous vacation trip – to Italy. You buy a bunch of guidebooks and make your wonderful plans. The Coliseum, the Michelangelo David, the gondolas in Venice. You may learn some handy phrases in Italian. It's all very exciting.

After months of eager anticipation, the day finally arrives. You pack your bags and off you go. Several hours later, the plane lands. The stewardess comes in and says, "Welcome to Holland."

"Holland?!" you say. "What do you mean, Holland?" I

signed up for Italy! I'm supposed to be in Italy. All my life I've dreamed of going to Italy.

But there's been a change in the flight plan. They've landed in Holland and there you must stay.

The important thing is that they haven't taken you to some horrible, disgusting, filthy place, full of pestilence, famine and disease. It's just a different place.

So you must go out and buy a new guidebook. And you must learn a whole new language. And you will meet a whole new group of people you would never have met.

It's just a different place. It's slower paced than Italy, less flashy than Italy. But after you've been there for a while and you catch your breath, you look around, and you begin to notice that Holland has windmills, Holland has tulips, Holland even has Rembrandts.

But everyone you know is busy coming and going from Italy, and they're all bragging about what a wonderful time they had there. And for the rest of your life you will say, "Yes, that's where I was supposed to go. That's what I had planned."

The pain of that will never, ever, go away, because the loss of that dream is a very significant loss.

But if you spend your life mourning the fact that you didn't get to Italy, you may never be free to enjoy the very special, the very lovely things about Holland.

Written by Emily Perl Kingsley

Of course as with all things, life goes on and all there is to be done is go and get on with it.

I quickly found out that with the diagnosis for Amy it now meant that we could set in motion the wheels of extra support that she was going to need when starting primary school in the September of that year.

This whole process was complicated and quite a battle, I began to realise that parents of special needs children are continually fighting for what should be given without question.

Help was set in place for Amy's start at school, social stories written to help her with the transition, and the general feeling from all staff who had worked with her was that she would cope well in the local village school, with her extra help. During the summer holidays plans for her to visit school prior to September were also arranged. Having come to terms with my Amy and the way she was, I resolved to making hers and Isabelle's happiness my priority. No two children could have been loved more than mine.

It was at this point that Sean started to sleep on the sofa downstairs, because I was getting so little sleep on the floor, I then shared my bed with both girls, Sean was quite happy about this. I believe it was actually a relief for him because when issues happened during the night he was downstairs, out of the way with the perfect excuse not to have to help.

Much of Amy's behaviour was hard to handle, even armed with the best knowledge to do so I still felt powerless in so many situations.

Isabelle was just a Mummy's girl, nobody else even seemed to be on her radar. She did watch Amy play and enjoyed a certain amount of their interaction, but really for her, she just needed me.

Before the summer holidays I had dates for all of my diagnostic tests. An MRI scan is, basically just boring and torture when you are desperate for the toilet!

The Evoked potentials test is harmless and none evasive so really no problem.

Lumbar puncture however is extremely unpleasant, and as scheduled to be the last of my tests, I was terrified about it. But in true Rosie style I decided I would go alone.

On the day, I arrived at what seemed to be an empty department, I checked my paperwork to ensure I was in the right place at the right time, and I was, so I sat and waited.

Eventually a very large, very black, man with a massive smile came through the door. He took me to the procedure room, talked through things with me at length. He was shocked I had come alone and he did everything possible to reassure me. The procedure itself was awful, it took about twenty minutes and during that time you cannot move, only a local anaesthetic is used so the feeling is weird, and painful, I couldn't wait to get out of there.

After a paracetamol and a short rest I was allowed home. Driving in a daze.

A short time after all the tests had been done I was sent an appointment to see my Neurologist. Once again I went alone, that was my decision though, I had offers from many good friends to take me, but no, it had to be just me.

It was July, an overcast day but not cold. I drove myself to my appointment in plenty of time.

Sitting anxiously in an overcrowded waiting room with wall to wall information leaflets about conditions nobody wants to have. The clock on the wall had a very loud tick but my fears were louder. My name was called, in I went, just as distant and mechanical as before, he beckoned me to sit, then just about as matter of fact as was possible, he delivered my diagnosis, all tests had returned a positive result, that was it, no more doubt, no more hoping against hope and wishing it all to be a mistake. I did have Multiple Sclerosis!

Chapter 15

On my return home, I told Sean, he hugged me loosely and then I asked him to roll me a smoke, I had not smoked for years.

I sat on the edge of my patio, alone with my roll up, I had no idea how I was going to do this, my mind was a wash with worry, grief and anger.

Sean did not have to work that day or night so I started on a box of wine and sent him to the shop for cigarettes.

The next day, as nursed my hangover, the world carried on as usual but I did not feel part of it anymore. I was in a solitary black hole.

It was summer holidays so during the days I kept myself busy with the girls, always doing something nice on every day, even as I pushed them on the swings at the park I wondered how long I would be able to still do that.

Even cooking their dinner I questioned how much longer I could do this.

I worried so much for their future, Sean was becoming increasingly detached from us.

The whole way through my lifetime alcohol had always been my escape mechanism, like a comfort blanket, the place I went to forget, it was needed as much as wanted, it only took a back seat when I was pregnant. At this time it was very much in the driving seat.

By day I was the best Mum I could be, by night I was pissed.

When you drink a massive quantity every day, your body adjusts and even after a considerable amount you can still function pretty well. The psychological damage is a different thing altogether.

Every morning you not only wake up feeling terrible physically, you also feel guilt and disgust, totally paranoid too, never wanting anyone to know the extent of your consumption, it becomes a painful secret and a powerful controller.

In the September of that year Amy started school at the Primary School in the village.

This was not an easy transition for her to make, autistic children hate even small changes, so this one was traumatic for her. Her teacher and the teaching assistant were both wonderful. We all did our best to make things as smooth and fun as it could be for her and she did, soon become to like school.

When Amy received her diagnosis at the hospital we were offered a course, reflections it was called, one morning a week for two hours over twelve weeks, as Sean had to stay and look Isabelle, Amy's teacher came with me on this course.

It was so valuable, filled in the gaps of my knowledge

about autism, giving fantastic advice and also meeting other parents going through the same difficulties.

At the end of the course, we were all really sad, some of us had become good friends, we exchanged numbers and vowed to keep in touch.

I felt I needed to do more, some of these parents were not coping at all well, I had an idea, decided to talk to my wonderful health visitor about it first.

With the help of my health visitor, I set up an Autism Support group, called Stars, for parents to get together and support each other and at the local sure start centre where I was able to hold my group, there was also lots for the children to do, play without being or feeling different.

I was very proud of my group, I channelled my energy into making it a success.

At the same time there was another support group, health visitor led, for parents and children with many differing special needs, that group was every Friday morning, I also became heavily involved with those meetings too.

As time went by, the amount of parents and children attending my Saturday Stars group started to drop, so I decided to merge it with the existing Friday morning group.

My health visitor was unable to be so involved due to other work commitments, so it was agreed that I was to run the two groups, together, every Friday. I gave this group everything I could. Baked cakes for every meeting and thoroughly enjoyed the diverse regulars that we had.

So many wonderful friends were made at that group, parents who felt isolated and alone in their worries for their children became united on those mornings.

All the time my alcohol consumption was off the scale! I felt guilt and shame every time I took Amy to school, or Belle to toddler group, I felt everyone knew, and I was being judged, which of course I wasn't because only I knew!

You are in a constant battle with yourself and the bottle, but the bottle always wins. A day without a drink was just unthinkable to me.

I relied on booze to get me through every day, most of my life had been that way, from the day of my father's funeral at the age of 13, alcohol was my saviour and I was back up to needing it more than ever.

I did not want this monster disease, I wanted a husband who was strong and there for me, I was on the whole externally great, internally wrecked.

Isabelle was two years old soon after Amy started school, having one daughter with autism had educated me to the early signs.

My Health Visitor came just to do a routine two year check on my precious Isabelle.

On finishing her assessment, she put down her pen, took

off her glasses and took my hand "you know don't you? Isabelle has just failed everything to do with communication, I am so sorry, I have to refer her"

I did already know, in my heart, but these words fell on top of me like boulders and crushed me to dust, once again.

Isabelle's referral came through quite quickly due to her sister's condition. After her educational psychologists appointment Belle was referred to the hospital for the same two day assessment that Amy had had.

On this two day hospital appointment, they concluded that yes, Isabelle showed all the signs of autism, but they were reluctant to diagnose her at such a young age and asked for another two day assessment to be scheduled for her when she was three years old.

At home we were very structured, I took photographs of everything form the car to Isabelle's shoes and socks. She was comforted by having a visual for what was to come next in her day, as the spoken words are most confusing for autistic children.

On the side of one kitchen unit I used a visual picture schedule for them both, with their names at the top of each list, Velcro laminated pictures planned their day for them and they both used it.

Many things made their day easier and I was learning all of the time.

MS continued to do its stuff! Making every day more

difficult, as I struggled with pain and fatigue. I could no longer walk great distances without a rest. Shopping was done online or not at all.

I began to resent Sean for his lack of empathy, common sense and willingness to help when needed.

He was in many ways simply just a third child, even my Health Visitor was of the opinion that he was actually autistic himself, which he refused to even listen to.

I seemed to be constantly wrapped up by an evil hangover, which by this time was joined by mysterious MS fuckery!

I just couldn't see any other way to cope, that wine was my constant, to get me through the day, I thought about it from the minute I woke, never touched a drop though until the girls were in bed, except weekends.

I did try and keep to just the one bottle during the week and it was never more than that if Sean was working a night shift, if he was at home though, there were times when it was closer to a box than a bottle even on a week day.

Sean never once questioned my drinking, talked about my feelings with all that was going on, or his to that matter.

Conversation between us was only about domestic matters and the girls. He still slept downstairs on the sofa and that too was never spoken about.

We never argued either though, our girls only knew happiness, I knew I could never destroy that, despite how trapped I now felt living with a man I had never even really loved properly.

I continued with the Friday group and it went from strength to strength, I was very proud of every one of those parents and humbled by many too.

When you have a child of special needs it opens up a door to an amazing world of parents whose strength is beyond compare and children who live lives of pain that would floor most adults but still they play and their laughter warmed the coldest day.

I organised a summer fete day just for our group and Christmas parties too, taking great pride in every event.

A positive in an otherwise difficult life, that I was struggling with more than I would admit.

One day, I was particularly low, the girls had been difficult and I was so fatigued I could barely think straight.

It was a Sunday so I started drinking early.

During that day and evening I put away best part of 5 bottles of wine all before collapsing around nine at night.

It was summer holidays and Sean was off work, when I woke Amy was stood next to the bed, I smiled at her then she said "Mummy are you poorly? In the night I couldn't wake you, I thought you were dead"

There was no better wakeup call than that. I looked down at myself, still in last night's clothes, I got out of bed and walked downstairs, "Sean you need to drive me to Northampton, there is somewhere I need to go" he looked puzzled "please don't ask questions just take me, I know the way to where I need to go".

I had researched their work, talked it over with my health visitor on many an occasion. We both knew I was an alcoholic.

Sean drove me and left me at CAN an association that deals with addiction and homelessness.

I walked into the small entrance, there was a window on the left, a kind lady looked up at me and I spoke

"I am an alcoholic, I do not want to drink anymore, can somebody help me please"

Take a seat in the waiting room, one of our team will see you shortly.

I began on my journey, one of the hardest I have ever had to take.

Rosie Fenton, alcoholic.

Chapter 16

I spoke at length with the counsellor, he was very easy to talk to, he gave me advice to help me, and I would get an appointment to see him again, every week for three weeks, after that my case would be re assessed, to see if further help was needed.

That very first day actually wasn't too hard because I had an extremely substantial hangover! The following day however was when the work really began. Although I never drank during the day, the drink I was to have later was always on my mind, somewhere safe, to take away the pain, and now that had been taken away, it was almost impossible to think of anything else.

That first week is a blur, not only had I the psychological battle of my life but also physically ill! I had the shakes, felt sick and had a high temperature. I can see why they say don't go 'cold turkey' but it was the only way for me, I took it hour by hour, to think any further than that was just too massive to comprehend!

Sean was very unsupportive and still drank lager at home in front of me, he did on one occasion when I was particularly low, offer to go to the village shop to buy me a bottle! I was strong, I said no. I felt at this point that the only person who understood my fight was my addiction counsellor, and I honestly do not think I could have done it without him.

Every single day was an intense struggle, against my will to drink, against multiple sclerosis and maintaining a calm organised life for my autistic daughters. I was completely alone in my feelings, like trying to climb an invisible mountain.

After my initial three weeks at counselling I was assigned to a more qualified counsellor, as my alcoholism was so deep routed, going right back to my childhood, after losing my father at thirteen, it was suggested that I would need extensive qualified help if I was to succeed. I still only took it day at a time "I will not drink today".

After about four counsellors it was decided I needed to be seen by a psychologist specialised in addiction. I needed to drive to Northampton for these appointments, the building I went to was used for serious addicts, safe needle disposal was provided and there were some very interesting characters. I have to say during my visits there, everyone was friendly and all carried their own story, this taught me a valuable lesson not to ever judge a person as you don't walk their path.

By this time I could see the wonderful positives of not drinking, no hangovers for one and the increase in my weight loss without drinking gallons of highly calorific wine! Mostly though, the guilt had gone and I did feel better without, so the girls benefitted too, hung-over Mummy was no fun at all!

I had many low points though where I knew how close I came to that bottle, my parents birthdays and the anniversaries of their deaths, Mother's and Father's Days were also tricky. Anything really that brought me down, took me closer to the edge. I stayed strong.

Also, driving to Northampton to see my psychologist was proving very difficult, too fatigued to drive that journey. The psychologist was very understanding and arranged for a room to be available for him to use for our appointments at the small local hospital. He made this journey to see only me, he was paramount to my success and he knew this as well as I did.

I already did all my shopping online, tried making sure there was time in every day for me to relax and sometimes a nap too Sean was becoming more and more distant, he could not comprehend how I felt, I did not expect him to, but as my husband I did at least expect him to try! He worked as many shifts as possible and when not working mostly fishing. He did the gardening and tended to his own fish pond and that was all.

When you have relied on something so heavily as I had done throughout almost my whole life, then it is no longer there, it's a scary lonely place you find yourself. You don't know who you are anymore. Nobody understood. This coupled with the MS made me emotionally slaughtered, I was clinically depressed, my Doctor was wonderful as always and we tried a number of anti-depressants to help me through. I had a volunteer lady come into see me, from a local charity that helped a number of families struggling for their own reasons. Her help was immense, sometimes she would occupy Belle for me to rest, did household chores and often we just talked. So valuable to me were these visits.

Thankfully through all of this my beautiful girls kept me strong, made me laugh uncontrollably, gave love in abundance and they were my reason for everything. I spent many hours making schedules for them and kept their lives in a routine the best way I could. With those two beautiful, amazing girls that somehow I had produced, we played, cuddled, laughed and cried together. We were in our own little autistic bubble by day. By night my fears were all I had.

I remained strong, I lapsed once with a bottle of red wine on my Mum's birthday, but strangely, I was glad I had, because I hated myself so much, and also felt so awful the next day, well more like bloody three days actually because I had not touched a drop for so long that it strengthened my resolve. I was too still losing weight and almost down to my target, what a fantastic feeling that was, my confidence was starting to return and clothes shopping became enjoyable!

Our lives were difficult, no family to help, facing a lot of ignorance where the Autism was concerned. Autism is emotionally draining. Multiple Sclerosis is extremely physically draining. We ticked along I thought, one day at a time. I seemed to be endlessly dealing with issues the girls had at School and Pre School. Socially they were just not equipped to deal with day to day playground situations, and it was heart-breaking having to watch them trying to understand this mad, crazy fucked up World we live in. For children who take every spoken word literally, the English Language, or rather the phrases we use within it, is ridiculous!

Home life did become somewhat easier when Isabelle started School. She had her own teaching assistant as did Amy, so I did not have to worry as they both had the extra support they needed. Having an entire day to myself, I could pace myself, rest when necessary, and on bad days do very little indeed. Primary Progressive MS as I had makes gradual deterioration to many different parts of your body and is different for everyone, I had good days and bad days at that point and with both girls at School I could manage this quite well.

My weight was now down to a healthy size 12, something I was extremely proud of. I still was not drinking, I was as proud as fuck about that!

It was those positives that my psychologist urged me to think of at times of despair, of which there were still many.

I was feeling far more in control of the alcohol, for the first time I was actually confident that I could live my life, happily and securely without it. Still to say "I will never drink again" was too scary. I had read many true life stories, about ordinary people from all walks of life, who had conquered an addiction to know that you have to be an addict to understand that.

I felt able to, and ready to say goodbye to my psychologist, he was less than enthusiastic about my decision, as he knew the depths of my hurt, by he respected my choice, gave me his mobile number should I feel the need to talk to hm. It had taken me two years to reach this point, it's a battle you never stop fighting and I had such enormous gratitude for all who helped me fight that evil disease of alcoholism.

I cried as I left that day, spikey little tears that carried a river of emotion with them. Also too was a smile on my face, I had done it, the one thing I had battled with for over three decades; I knew I was lucky to be alive. I was so immensely proud of myself.

Rosie Fenton, recovering alcoholic.

Chapter 17

Amy and Isabelle were happy children, you never feel a love so complete as the one you feel for you own child. So for me, contentment and tolerance came with their happiness, and there was nothing that I wouldn't do for my children.

Sean and I by this time however were not living as man and wife really, he slept on the sofa and we had no sexual activity what so ever! This didn't bother me particularly, certainly not as much as it should have! but although we shared no intimacy, we also had no animosity against each other either, so the girls never heard an argument or cross word because there were none.

Sometimes, I would sit and wonder how beautiful it would be if we were crazy about each other, madly in love and enjoying great sex together, I couldn't remember a time when that had ever happened, I don't think it did. We had reached a point where sex was no longer an option, Sean was more like a brother, he was the father of my children and I cared for him a great deal, but to have sex with him, fuck me no! The thought actually made me shudder, which was wrong on so many levels, but it was how I felt.

As far as the girls' welfare was concerned I could not leave them with Sean without worrying for them. For one example I had an MRI scan appointment to attend one afternoon, Sean was left with both girls, instructions left for their dinner, although I said I should be back by then. On arriving for my test I was told there was a long unavoidable delay, the department was in the basement of the hospital with no mobile phone signal. I was there for over three hours, it was dark when I came, I was cold and hungry. I picked up my phone to 12 texts all from Sean asking where I was. Exasperated I phoned him, the girls had had nothing to eat or drink since I left, he had no common sense at all, no logic that should have told him that although I hoped to be back, I was clearly running late and the children needed their dinner. After three hours and an annoying MRI to then know my girls had not even had basic care, I was furious, I drove home saying "twat" repeatedly, loudly!

Despite having a lack of desire for my husband, his inability to take responsibility, and him being more of a burden than a support. I could never have left, broken our family and our children's hearts. My own wish for someone to love me properly and for me to love and be in love with, took a firm backseat to the girls emotional and physical well-being. I assumed Sean felt the same. He had not for years, tried to instigate any sexual behaviour between us, or expressed a concern as to why we didn't. My understanding was that he was content the way we were, he always seemed happy. Communication was not Sean's strong point by far, so, any discord he did feel, he would not have told me about.

I was of the understanding that as long as Amy and Isabelle were happy, Sean and I would remain solid. I resigned myself to spending the rest of my life without a good old shagging! Small price to pay I thought.

On the approach towards Christmas that year I was finding my MS increasing difficult. Terrible fatigue haunted me by day and insomnia by night. I suffered with terrible headaches, all day, every day, it was so draining. Numbness and pain were with me at most times too. All my energies were absorbed by the girls, at this point they did not know about my condition, or indeed their own, I felt them too young for this information. I too had not completely accepted my diagnosis. So I kept life as normal as possible for them.

It never occurred to me for one second that Sean was actually unhappy with our life the way it was. Until for no reason, the weekend before Christmas, I thought he was being uncharacteristically cold with me and then I noticed he had taken his wedding ring off! I was completely taken aback by this, I kept calm, said nothing and decided it best I approach the situation after the children were in bed. This was what I did. I asked Sean why he had taken his ring off and he flatly refused to talk about it, I asked him repeatedly, got mostly a none verbal shrug as response. Exasperated by the lack of communication from him I simply went to bed.

Sunday morning was more of the same, I was ignored by Sean unless the children were involved. I made the day completely normal for Amy and Isabelle, so they were blissfully unaware of how drastically their young lives were going to be changed.

Once again after they were sleeping I tried to talk to Sean, he just ignored me again, I begged him to tell me what was wrong, but as the previous evening he refused to shed any light on the situation. I became annoyed eventually and took myself off into the conservatory to wrap over thirty Christmas presents for the group party on the Tuesday, with my plan B CD on as loud as I could without waking my children. Allsorts was running through my mind, Sean's ring had never left his finger since the day it was I put it there. After completing the wrapping, and that was quite a task for tired arms and hands, I had naturally expected that my husband would have been helping me. I asked him one last time to talk to me, he simply turned away. I went to bed.

On the Monday morning was planned our annual big Christmas supermarket shop. I was up with the girls as normal, even breakfast and dressing to go out can be a trial with two very young autistic children. We were nearly ready when I noticed Sean sorting out some clothes, clothes he rarely wore, he still had not spoken to me, I took a step back as it occurred to me "My God you're not leaving are you?" Without looking at me, he said yes but after Christmas, neither of us noticed Amy standing in the doorway behind us, she started crying immediately, asking if Daddy was leaving, I was furious, really fucking furious!

I pacified Amy then told Sean "upstairs now" I was livid, I remember clearly exactly what I said "Whatever your bloody reasons are I no longer care, I swear on their lives I have never once been unfaithful to you, I have begged you all weekend to talk to me when the girls were sleeping and this is what you do! You are a pathetic waste of a man and I will never forgive you for this, you've broken that little girls heart because you haven't even got the gumption to talk to me at the proper time, you can go today, we are going to Sainsbury's and when we get back I want you gone!" I never raised my voice.

I made a girly shopping trip sound like fun and both girls happily climbed in the car. I walked around that shop in a blur, spent a fortune, saying yes to everything the girls asked for. How was I going to make this okay for them? I didn't cry or let them see that I was rocked to my very core by what had happened that morning, just before Christmas, my foundations were damaged but the terrible thing was I genuinely felt a kind of relief. My loveless marriage was over, my children were my world though so I had to focus on what I could do to make this as easy for them as possible.

I explained in the car that Daddy had decided he would like to live somewhere else, and that often Daddy's would do that, but he still loved them very much and they would see him a lot of the time. Amy shed a few tears but I managed to make it all sound so positive, they accepted it remarkably well.

When we got home, Sean was gone, most of his clothes and other personal possessions too. I made toast.

The rest of the day, in a complete foundation free state, I made everything as normal as possible for the girls. Kept positive and answered their questions as honestly as I could. We had a lovely day, strange and unexpected, but really quite fine. I had no contact from the girl's father for the rest of that day at all.

The following day was the group Christmas party day. I

organised the whole thing, I behaved as normal and the party was a wonderful success. Some gorgeous, very challenged children came to the group, this day, their faces were a picture as Father Christmas came through the door with three massive sacks of presents, each carefully chosen for each child. It was a very special day indeed. As we cleared away afterwards I told a couple of the Mum's I was closest to, but kept it short and brief.

It still didn't seem real. I could not comprehend how the father of my children, Mr Weak and Pathetic, had planned to leave us. I dealt with everything, he wouldn't even telephone the Doctor's to make an appointment because that would mean communication with somebody, his teeth were rotting in his mouth as I had said he must deal with that himself. I even made his pack lunch for work! But he had planned this over God knows how long and all on his own.

My life had shifted in a completely unexpected direction, I made the girls priority, I never shed a tear. When on Christmas Eve I finally got a text from the girl's father asking when he could see them, I gave him my carefully thought out answer, that he could see them whenever he wished. When he came round later that day, he knocked the front door, I opened it and as natural as I could be, and simply said "Hi, would you like a cup of tea?"

We never spoke of him leaving or his reasons for why, we just acted as normal for the children, I asked him to come and spend Christmas Day with us, which he did albeit later than planned, so the girls had to wait to open their presents, also with a stinking hangover, and he fell asleep after Christmas dinner! He left mid-afternoon of his own accord. Amy and Isabelle seemed happy, but were confused and quiet when he left.

On that Christmas evening I sat alone, I annoyed and confident that I could do this on my own. My illness, my children, my world would be fine.

I never shed a tear.

In the days that followed, I sorted all money issues, telephoned all the people that needed to know and most importantly, gave as much of myself to the girls as I possibly could. How he could hurt them in this way was beyond me, but to mend them and keep them happy and secure was not.

I gave the girl's father unlimited access, but as he was only renting a room at a friend's house, most contact involved him coming into my home. He never organised to take them out, I would do that for them and he would take them. In those initial weeks it was very difficult indeed to maintain a pleasant exterior for Amy and Isabelle, when I just wanted to scream at him.

During this time however, Multiple Sclerosis continued with its work and I was badly hit with fatigue. My strength was depleting, fine dexterity going and I had toileting issues. All this caused me to sit back and take a long look at myself and how I could make my life simpler, so that my strength was conserved for the children.

So, with a heavy heart I handed over the running of my

support group to a gentleman that I believed would be a perfect replacement, unfortunately that did not turn out to be the case, all the money others and myself had raised for play equipment and art materials for the children, was quickly squandered on adults refreshments, something I refused to do, always providing refreshments myself and leaving a tin for those who could afford to, to make a contribution. I had to sit back and watch all my hard work turn to dust. The group is no more.

That evening, I did have tears, I cried for the loss of that very special group and every hour that I had spent building it.

Chapter 18

Multiple Sclerosis is a very unpredictable, relentless beast. No two patients are the same, no set organisation of progression; it does what it wants, where and when it wants. Extreme fatigue does affect a lot of us though and is very hard to explain to people with no knowledge of the condition just how debilitating this can be. With all these physical symptoms also very often comes the feeling loss, you mourn the old you, feeling worthless and useless as everyday tasks become increasingly difficult.

Autism too is a baffling beast all of its own. Again, very different from child to child. They find it sometimes impossible to verbalise their emotions. They need a rigid daily schedule with good prior warning of changes. Repetition of all requests is essential for them to grasp sometimes very mundane tasks such as getting dressed. They are particular about food not readily accepting new foods. All of their emotions are exaggerated. Very often the spoken words are misunderstood as they emphasise the incorrect word within a sentence.

Our home was lovely; it was not large although the garden was! I decorated the conservatory first, changed some photos around and bought a new bed. Money was tight, but as I didn't drink, ever go out nor buy take away food, so I could manage with what we had and still save some cash for these small changes that made our house more of our home and not as it was when the father of my children lived with us too.

Life was certainly not easy, but the extra special bond that grew between the three of us was so wonderful, it more than made up for the difficulties of being a single Mum, in her forties with the same fucking awful shit disease that had taken her parents and the challenges of Autism.

Everything we did, we did together. Picnics and parks. Meal times round the table where we talked and laughed. Having nobody else to look after meant all of my time was theirs. When Amy and Isabelle were at school, that was my time for chores and grabbing a nap when possible. So they returned to a clean house and a Mummy who could not wait to see them.

I started the girls at swimming lessons on a Saturday morning, difficult for Isabelle to start off with as she hated water on her face, but she rapidly progressed. Amy loved it from day one. I loved watching them so much, a valuable sport that I could rest whilst they did it. This also gave a routine to our weekends and Sundays were our pyjama days.

The girl's father remained a regular visitor, usually once a week, but it was always at our home, very often I would cook for him too, I thought this a good thing to maintain, for the girls to see both their parents together without discord. It did however mean the only time I had for myself was during the school day, mostly doing household stuff, or watching a movie after they had gone to bed.

I was lonely and I was depressed. I became a master at

turning down invitations, making excuses for people not to visit me. I did like to maintain the children's friendships, though, as it's not easy for them to make friends, so I was always keen to have their friends here.

During this time, I had countless moments of extreme joy with my children. I also had many nights of tears and despair. Having MS myself made me only too aware of the pain and struggle that both my parents went through, most of which I was completely oblivious to as a child. I think what struck me most though was what my poor Mum had been through, to have to nurse a sick husband, only to lose him in her early thirties and then to be handed the same sentence with two children to care for. To then have to spend her last few years at the hands of strangers albeit in her own home. The enormity of that I still to this day struggle to comprehend.

Myself, I have days still where I feel so very angry, how unfair life seems to have been for me. But then when those moments come they are usually followed by feelings of gratitude, I have the two most amazing daughters who drive me through my pain to sunshine again.

I went to great lengths to make sure in that first year that Amy and Isabelle had a good relationship with their father. We even holidayed together. Spending a week with the husband who walked away from you, believe me is very fucking difficult! Never was I so pleased to get home. The children had a lovely time and with that as my aim I had to call it a success regardless of how hard it was.

Even on holiday though, the girl's father exhibited a catalogue of stupidity that actually put the girls in danger. I was reading my book one day on a beach in Scotland, the girls and their Dad were down in the sea, a fair distance from where I was. I looked up from reading regularly to see all was well, then I noticed Amy going off in a different direction, still in the sea but quite some distance for the other two, I stood up watching and panicking as the gap between them widened. My weak MS legs carried me quickly as anything to Amy. Their father failed to see the danger in this situation.

There were numerous occasions such as that one, making me feel anxious whenever the girls were alone with their Dad, that was another reason for me being happy for them to have their time with him in their own home with just the odd trip to the park or swimming.

This first year on my own with the girls was incredibly hard, I had no support from Tom and his wife at all, my dearest friends Kate and India were always there for me, but even knowing that, I would actively seek solitude. Multiple Sclerosis strips you of many things and for me, my confidence was one of them, and I had precious little of that anyway! Being a single parent in any circumstances is a hard one.

I adapted to being the lone parent quite well I thought though and hoped that my parents could somehow see me, and were proud.

I had no interest in finding another partner or trying any kind of reconciliation with the girl's father. The opposite in fact, I embraced my single status, changed my name back to my maiden name and was good at being my own boss. The MS was the only ball and chain around my core holding me back.

Amy and Isabelle thrived at school with their own teaching assistants. Of course there were issues and behaviour wise my darling Amy was the testing one, but as she grew I learned to handle her much better. Isabelle was never a problem, an anxious little child, sensitive and with a beautiful nature, I worried about her as I knew expressing her emotions was still very difficult. Their father took no interest in their schooling, never attended a single parent's evening or meetings concerning their special educational needs.

I organised all their parties myself, wonderful ones too. There was rarely a cross word between their father and myself, but I had absolutely no respect for him and as a father he was spineless. I made everything very easy for him, not for his reward but for my children. They really were my world.

In the middle of that first year I had to have a cataract implant, due to an old injury from my drinking days. It was my friends that helped me through this, as I could not drive for a few weeks. Friends took charge of taking the girls to and from school for me, their father did as little as possible. He wasn't even in the country for one of Isabelle's Birthdays!

I kept my weight low. I drank no alcohol, despite the wish to, being so overpowering at times, it felt like I was drowning, but still I didn't drink.

At what stage exactly I am not completely sure, the girl's father found himself a girlfriend and with this his time for his own children became even less frequent. When he was with them, he spent majority of his time texting on his phone. This infuriated me! What a wanker, first he fucks off, when things get tough and now he had his perfect single life just playing Daddy on the odd occasion when it suited him. I decided to take a step back. If he wanted to see his children then he would have to make arrangements and actually do something with them.

Although my children were everything to me and always would be, I started to crave being a women again, having a man in my life. Looking for any kind of relationship with a chronic illness is not easy, then throw in two autistic children it is almost impossible. However we do now in our modern day lives have the wonders of social networking, with all its good points and bad ones in equal measures, it does allow conversation and friendships to grow without leaving the house!

So, Rosie Fenton, singleton on the pull was born!

Chapter 19

I had my house beautiful by now and exactly how I wanted it to be. Amy and Isabelle both settled at school and both with the extra help they needed.

So I could for the first time turn some of the attention upon myself. I was quite happy being single and certainly didn't need a man, but just felt I would like one, the right one, should he exist.

Now on the grounds that the girls had never spent a night with their Dad since he left and being autistic I was extremely limited on what I could do. Also, having a chronic illness and two autistic children, didn't make me a great catch! The chronic illness destroyed my confidence and without alcohol I was still very unsure of who I was supposed to be.

In my situation, social networking was both the greatest asset and the most dangerous disaster all in one screen! My friends list was large, so I had a little browse of potentials, and embarked on some flirtatious conversations with an undesirable who very soon got the bullet!

A few unremarkable males crossed my path, but nobody made me feel any pull of desire or depth. I pretty much gave up really, I quite honestly wasn't that bothered, being single has some amazing advantages and the girls were great company when they were at home with me, until.

A comment on a status of mine, on my regular networking site, turned my head, so I delved a little deeper into the profile of this chap, I couldn't even think how we became friends in the first place, so it was starting a fresh with someone new. John, was a few years younger than me, a couple of inches shorter too, he owned nothing of any value and it's fair to say had not had the greatest upbringing. We started to talk online regularly, he was different to the rest.

During these conversations I was completely honest, about my MS, the limitations the entailed, the children and their extra special needs, my recovery alcoholic state and all the demons from my past that still influenced decisions that I made and feelings that I felt.

John too was equally as honest, good and bad, he hid nothing. I loved his openness, the fact that we could talk on a non-sexual level for hours. Most men fail miserably at that, exposing their intentions wide open. John was different.

We communicated on this level for quite a few weeks, before I finally found the courage to invite him round for a coffee one morning. John had no car so, the very morning I asked if he would like to come round for coffee, he was in my car, less than three miles door to door, we were soon at my house. I was incredibly nervous although I am absolutely sure he could not tell.

We sat on my old green sofa in the conservatory and talked, I made it clear that I had no available cash, taking that incentive away if it was ever there. The more we talked the more I felt, there is something about this man, I couldn't tell you what, just something, that touched me, something I liked very much. When I took him home we had a single kiss. I touched my lips on the way home and smiled.

John and I over the next three weeks, spent more and more time together. I did not introduce him to my girls as I thought it way too early for that. We got on well, some of our likes differed, music being the main one, but we made a connection.

Once again my past reared its ugly head and I started to feel insecure, my mood swings were out of my control. John, bless him was dealing with some recent difficulties of his own, so he decided it would be best if we didn't go any further. I was quite frankly devastated, in those three short weeks, I had grown strong feelings for this man, but, I had to respect his decision, so we ended, before we really started.

It was just before Christmas so I had lots to take my mind off John. Our annual Panto trip. Christmas day was perfect, Sean did come and see the girls but rushed back to his girlfriend pretty quickly, which pleased the three of us. Despite my best efforts, their bond with their father was lessoning due to his lack of interest and his preoccupation with his phone when they were together, children are very perceptive.

I was however very poorly over that Christmas, my MS was firing at me from all directions and I also had a stomach bug, I lost nearly a stone. With nobody to help with the girls that was hard, but we got through, the three of us together. Then I found a lump in my breast.

The very next day I saw my GP, she agreed there was a

lump, instantly referred and within a fortnight I was sitting in a crowded waiting room, full of ladies all with the same tense, terrified expression I knew I had. The mammary gram itself was not as painful as I expected, waiting to see the consultant for the result was fucking awful though! The thoughts that race through your mind at a time like that is horrific. I sat there, on my own, all thoughts with my precious girls and what on earth would happen to them should anything happen to me. I had all those thought already because of my chronic illness, but this was different, far more intense.

My name was called by nurse, I think I held my breath for the entire length of that corridor, and didn't actually breathe, until I heard those words, all was fine. On my way home, I really wanted to call John, I decided against it and bought a celebratory brownie instead!

From time to time, I would text John, I never got a reply. I closed my social networking page, I just felt I wanted to shut myself away, from everything except my gorgeous kids. My monster MS continued to trick me with gravity and always with pain. My girls remained the centre of my world, they were my all, my strength, my sunshine, my reason for everything.

Through everything, I kept my weight down, never touched a drop of drink, even on special anniversary's, such as my Dad's birthday, which was always so very painful. I kept as much of my monster's symptoms from the girls, although they did know Mummy was poorly, details I tried not to show. For the first time, I felt very proud of myself, what I had accomplished and how well

I coped. Well, most of the time, we all fuck up occasionally.

This fuck up though I'm glad I made, I had promised myself to text John no more, then one day in March, at a weak moment, I did send him a text. I did get a reply.

John and I started talking again, occasionally at first, then more frequently. Some of John's issues had been resolved and he felt stronger and more able to deal with mine. April 11th that year we got back together. Taking things very slowly.

It is safe to say that my relationship with John was not plain sailing. We kept it just the two of us for the first few months and what a bloody rollercoaster it was! Two very passionate people, both strong minded and both strong willed, with a hell of a lot to deal with. We could not go out on dates as the girls would stay with nobody. My mood swings were horrific and my insecurity even more so! He certainly had his hands full and had a few vices himself that caused us grief. We were very up and down for really most of that year.

Amy and Isabelle were introduced to John in the Summer Holidays of that year, he was Mummy's friend to them and when he stayed over, he slept on that old green sofa in the conservatory where our first conversation took place.

When you live in constant pain, decision making, emotional overload and insecurity rule your thoughts. Whilst with the girls I could control this to a point that kept their life in a level, safe and happy environment.

With John however this was very different and every little thing would throw me over the edge. This was hard for us both and during that year we were on and off so many times I lost count. Sometimes short breaks and occasionally longer ones.

By this time however I was in love with John and he with me. Even apart our thoughts were often of each other, we had so much to deal with though, and I feared our love would not be strong enough. We were apart for all our Birthdays and Christmas that year.

With my girls though everything was wonderful, they continued to blossom at school, at home mostly, as long as we kept to our routines all was good. Their father's input remained sporadic and not a patch on what they deserved!

John and I both seemed to bounce back to each other, and every time it was as though we had never been apart. Slowly but surely we strengthened our love for each other.

Amy and Isabelle were too starting to become very fond of John, and we dealt with our time apart so well that the girls were in no way hurt by it. They loved having him here and did not worry when he wasn't.

John was always extremely understanding about my condition, he worried for me and helped in any way he could, whenever he could, only becoming annoyed when I tried to be independent when really I was too tired to do so. Any slight cross word instantly made me feel unloved, I hated how my emotions were so fragile, this was often the root of our evils.

I quite simply went from feelings of euphoria to desperation within a second from only a tiny trigger. Understandably this was hard for John and on so many instances I pushed him away when really all I wanted to do was pull him closer.

It was during one of our fall outs that I lapsed, I talked my neighbour into sparing me a bottle of wine. Decent white, of a good strength. Once my girls were safely in bed, out came my glass, my favourite glass, my quality opener still at the back of my cutlery draw. I looked at the three items in front of me, and swiftly removed the cork, poured half a glass, and drank it down without a breath. The rest of the bottle quite quickly followed. Instantly I hated myself.

Chapter 20

Following the drinking episode, John was furious, and quite rightly so. It was however, just the one, the one bottle. How I felt emotionally and physically afterwards was all I needed to ensure it was just a lapse. The last one, the final time I would drink, I hope to maintain this and will always, with everything that I am, ensure it was my last encounter with the evil liquid that overpowered me for too long.

Against all odds by the summer of that year we were stronger than we had ever been and planned a family holiday to a cottage in Scotland. It was in the school holidays and we were all very excited about the trip. Although I worried, about just about everything! I worried about worrying!

We set off early the day of the holiday, we shared the driving, both girls were very good as were our two dogs that also came with us. When we arrived the cottage was beautiful and in the most perfect location. I think I was more excited than the children!

The problem was, the girls and I, and their father in the early years had done cottage holidays in so many places, but because of their autism our basic routine remained the same. For John of course, this was his first trip away with us, and without realising it, I carried on the way we always did, mealtimes and day trips were all within our normal holiday boundaries, John felt quite left out.

John and I had a few disagreements that did not affect the children at all. I however, felt distraught, this holiday, in my head was to be absolutely and completely perfect! Just the four of us together was going to make it that way for me, my foundations became very shaky as I came to believe that John did not want to be with us. This was not the case at all, but that was what my head made of it.

So in true Rosie style, completely exaggerated and not at all necessary, but my insecurity took over and on the Thursday I took John to the local, very small town, gave him £130 and told him make your own way home!

John did not want to go, I left him no choice!

Amy and Isabelle were obviously confused; I quickly turned their attention to the beach and what a wonderful girly day it was going to be. Inside, once again I was lost. My reactions to a simple misunderstanding had resulted in our holiday being broken. Scars from the past don't heal well, and really deep ones never do.

For the rest of the holiday I made it imperative that my daughters enjoyed every minute, and they did. I coped with my own fears with remarkable control for their benefit. Fearing of course that for John and I we had reached the end of our journey. I did receive an odious message on his return home, all I could expect or deserve really.

After only a few days of being home, I did see John, briefly though, we argued, I panicked and told him I never wanted to see him again. My heart was in tiny, unrecognisable pieces. I picked them up, but they didn't quite fit together.

The Girls Birthdays both fell in the next few months, also my own. Plenty to keep me occupied making their days as special as was humanly possible. Birthdays are memories children take with them into adulthood, along with holidays and other little random events. So birthdays were a massive deal for me, spending every penny I could afford and with great attention to detail. This year for both girls was no exception, and although extremely exhausted, I was proud of myself for all I had done on my own. Their father gave them money.

My own birthday however was most unremarkable; I didn't care, well, maybe, just a bit.

Mid November came a text I was not expecting to receive, from John, my heart did a flying leap! We talked, we both realised our feelings had not changed at all. I was still in love with John and John was in love with me, the only place we should be is together. On the 1st of December, with total conviction from both sides, John and I were one, we both wanted forever.

Mostly I think we floated through December, still in shock to both be where we thought we had lost. Differences were settled quickly, although we were still both learning, we knew being together was meant to be and being apart was torture.

Christmas was all for the girls, John and I both completely agreed on that, buying only token presents for each other and some amazing surprises for the girls. We ate only party food, so no long stint at the cooker for Rosie, can say I was not sorry about that! I told John he was more than most welcome to drink, I didn't mind, I really didn't either, just wanted him to enjoy his

Christmas too, but, no, he was adamant that he would never drink in my presence. This spoke volumes to me, how committed he so obviously was to me, I fell deeper in love with him every day.

The girl's father gave them money and a token gift, and did not come Christmas Day.

John did go home for short periods of time over that Christmas time but majority of the time, including New Year's Eve he was with us. We didn't do anything special, just spent time together, the four of us and for me this was the happiest I had ever felt.

Yes I had pain every day, yes I was exhausted all of the time, yes I still hated every obstacle that MS put in my way, but, I was gloriously happy with my children and the amazing man I knew I wanted in my life forever. Whether or not this will be the case, only time will tell.

So many times, probably daily I thought of my dear parents and their suffering. My father was an amazing man who had the intellect and humour to captivate a room. Some of this he gave to me, I feel proud and blessed to have had the gift of a wonderful father, yes taken too soon, but many people never have that.

Thoughts of my wonderful Mum give me strength at weak times, as now I fully understand what a courageous, selfless woman she was, and how lucky I am to have been given her example.

When you have been physically and mentally abused, with inner strength and self-belief, you can conquer your fears, but it takes time, to fully understand the wonder of your own strength to survive.

Addiction is an evil thing and very misunderstood, but with the right help and determination you can overcome anything, if your desire to do some is strong enough.

I find myself now, at forty five years old, fighting a chronic illness that will only worsen, not alone though. This man by my side will be right there, no doubt, no question, our love is deep enough for us to fight it together. With us are two quite remarkable young girls, who make me proud every day, I look at their faces and burst with love.

My life is whole and complete and happy.

Rosie Fenton in a world of love, happiness and hope.

The Final Chapter

I sat on my bed, bereft, he was gone, my Daddy, my best friend my everything. I felt completely alone, I love Mum so much but Daddy was different. I was too young to not have my Daddy, he was taken too soon, how would I live the rest of my life without him.

The grief swallowed me whole, it was only three days ago and I could close my eyes and still smell him, feel his touch and hear his words.

I could never understand how such a great man could be given such an evil disease, why, I had asked myself that question a million times.

Every wish, stirring every Christmas Pudding, was for Daddy to get better.

I still could not really comprehend it. He was actually gone, gone forever. I had not slept since. I cried alone mostly.

Never having the chance to say goodbye was the very worst, I would be forever afraid without him.

I went downstairs, into the kitchen with the pale blue painted walls, and then I remembered, in cookery lessons that week we had made cakes, simple plain cupcakes with chocolate chips, into the pantry I went, there it was on its own, the last cake, I saved it for Daddy. Why such a small thing gave me the flood of tears it did I will never know, it was at that moment that I broke, and never properly mended.

So goodbye my darling Daddy and I hope you know that

for you I saved The Last Cake.

The End

Printed in Great Britain
by Amazon.co.uk, Ltd.,
Marston Gate.